The Modern Soccer Coach Pressing

Gary Curneen

First Printing: 2017
ISBN 978-1-365-79789-7
Modern Soccer Coach LLC
625 Berwick Street
Bakersfield, CA 93311
www.modernsoccercoach.com
Special discounts are available on quantity purchases by corporations, associations, educators, and other. For details, contact the publisher at gary@modernsoccercoach.com.
Inside images (as marked): ©Academy Soccer Coach

Acknowledgements

There have been a number of people who have assisted in the process of putting this book together. Firstly, I want to thank all the coaches and tactical analysts who contributed their work including Liam Bramley, Neil Adair, Tim Palmer, Gavin MacLeod, Karl Matchett, Colin Trainor, Johannes Harkins, Judah Davies, and Ally McBain. In addition, the work of Jed Davies, Pedro Mendonca, Rene Maric and Xavier Tamarit has inspired me to look a lot deeper into the tactical world and re-evaluate my own ideas after reading their work. I urge all coaches to read their work.

I must give special thanks to David Belfort who assisted in the design process with Modern Soccer Coach. David has been an excellent resource as we have begun working on our brand and his knowledge, feedback, and hard work have been incredibly helpful.

A special thank you must also go to Anson Dorrance for his time, energy, and willingness to talk freely regarding his system and coaching philosophy. He is an inspiration to so many coaches with his work on the field, but his humility and enthusiasm is what inspired me after meeting him.

Alongside the research and writing, I have attempted to use exercises, training methods, and playing systems at California State University, Bakersfield. The players have always been open to new ideas and have produced a consistent work rate, both on and off the field. A huge thanks to our staff. Clifton Bush, Tori Ornela, Donna Fishter, and Brandon Mikulecky who have challenged and supported one another throughout the process and have helped the program and myself get better every day.

Without the help of Erin Curneen and Janice Lentz, I would not have been able to put this book together. Their work and dedication, as well as their patience, throughout the process has been invaluable and greatly appreciated.

Last but not least, thank you to every coach who is sharing information and contributing positively to the coaching world. Without people being open and willing to share ideas, the profession would not be moving at the speed in which it is. Please continue to keep the ball rolling!

Academy Soccer Coach

Academy Soccer Coach is a company that provides digital solutions for coaches at every level of the game. Our coaching software enables coaches, clubs and professional organizations to plan and prepare their sessions remotely from anywhere in the world.

Academy Soccer Coach works with the following professional clubs and organizations:

Fulham FC, West Ham United FC, Stoke FC, Newcastle United FC, Crystal Palace FC, Portland Timbers Sporting Kansas City, National Soccer Coaches Association of America, US Soccer (Women's), The Irish Football Association, The Professional Footballers Association, and many more.

For more information on Academy Soccer Coach and the services we provide please visit www.academysoccercoach.com

Table of Contents

Chapter 1 – To Press or Not to Press..1

Modern Principles of Defending...2

Hold It Right There..4

Embrace the Process...5

Chapter 2 – The 'Why' Before the 'How'...7

Establish a Model of Play...8

How to Develop a Model of Play...11

Aligning Your Playing Model to Pressing.................................12

Defensive Organization..13

Low Block, Medium Block or High Press?...............................14

Summary..19

Chapter 3 – Pressing Player Profiles..21

Methodology Matters...23

High Pressing Player Characteristics...26

Exercise One..30

Exercise Two..32

Exercise Three...34

Exercise Four...37

Exercise Five..39

Exercise Six..41

Exercise Seven...43

Exercise Eight..45

Exercise Nine...47

Summary..49

Chapter 4 – Pressing Warm-Ups..51

Intensity Drivers...52

Pressing Warn-Up Coaching Principles....................................52

Exercise One..53

Exercise Two..55

Exercise Three...57

Exercise Four..59

Exercise Five..61

Exercise Six...63

Exercise Seven...65

Summary..66

Chapter 5 – Gegenpressing...**67**

Why Do It? 68

How Do You Coach It? 69

Exercise One..73

Exercise Two..75

Exercise Three...77

Exercise Four..79

Exercise Five..81

Exercise Six...83

Exercise Seven...85

Exercise Eight..87

Exercise Nine...89

Exercise Ten..91

Summary..93

Chapter 6 – Medium Block..**95**

Why Use a Medium Block? 97

How to Beat the Block? 99

Exercise One...101

Exercise Two...103

Exercise Three..105

Exercise Four..108

Exercise Five..110

Exercise Six..112

Exercise Seven...114

Summary...115

Chapter 7 – High Pressing..**117**

Starting Positions..117

Different Systems, Different Solutions..120

High Press Killers..125

Exercise One..127

Exercise Two..129

Exercise Three..131

Exercise Four..133

Exercise Five..135

Exercise Six..137

Exercise Seven..140

Exercise Eight..141

Exercise Nine..143

Exercise Ten..145

Summary..146

Chapter 8 – Characteristics of High Pressing Coaches..**147**

Jurgen Klopp..148

Anson Dorrance..155

Mauricio Pochettino..165

Brendan Rodgers..171

Chapter 9 – Getting the Details Right..**183**

Recruitment..183

Communication..184

Evaluating Your Press..186

Measuring It..188

Coaches Without an Analysis Department..188

Practice Design..189

Adding Practice Variability..193

Meeting Physical Demands of the Game..193

Feedback..195

Individual Video Analysis..196

Summary..197

Final Thoughts..**199**

Recommended Reading..**200**

1
To Press or Not to Press

Pressing is one of the latest trends that has taken the football world by storm. Every fan wants their team to do it, every team fears playing against it. Of course, there is a very good reason for the excitement. When teams get pressing right, it can be absolutely devastating. It has the ability to expose defenders in possession, send midfielders into areas that they do not particularly want to receive the ball, and frustrate opposing forwards who are reduced to chasing lost causes as they are starved of the ball for long periods of time. Above all however, it can create waves of momentum and confidence that can win teams games and strike dread in their competition.

Pressing, as we will explore throughout this book, can be an extremely complex system of play. There are many different ways to press in a variety of playing systems. However, the definition is quite simple. Without possession of the ball, the team works to win it back with an extreme sense of urgency. It is not one individual act but a unified movement by an entire team, including or in some cases, especially the forwards. It is a fast and furious defensive strategy aimed at catching opposition players off-guard. There are three different types of pressure based on the position of the field in which it occurs. The easiest way to understand and explain this tactic to players is by dividing the pitch into thirds. High pressing is in the attacking third of the field. Mid block pressing takes place in the second third and midfield area. Low block is pressure in the defensive third of the field.

Of course, the system itself is not new. Pressing has been around for a long time with Russian coach, Victor Maslov, credited with introducing it in the 1960s with his Dynamo Kyiv. The great Rinus Michels took it and then created 'Total Football' with Holland in the 1974 World Cup. Suddenly, on the world stage people stood up and took notice. Arrigo Sacchi revolutionised defending with his AC Milan team of the 1990's. With the help of the old offside rules, his back four squeezed high and compressed midfield areas, and together with attacking players like Gullit and Van Basten, fired them to domestic and European glory. Over a decade later, it was Argentinian coach, Marcelo Bielsa, who took Sacchi's model and developed it into 'vertical football' - a fast paced, furious system designed to exhaust the opposition. If Michels, Sacchi, and Bielsa helped develop modern day pressing, it was Pep Guardiola and Barcelona who have taken it to another level. On the women's side Anson Dorrance made aggressive pressure a hallmark in his UNC teams who have won over 800 games, including a remarkable twenty-one national championships in thirty-six seasons. These coaches may not be credited for inventing pressing, but they deserve enormous respect for developing it to the demands of the game itself and creating a template that today's coaches are using and adapting to their respective teams and leagues.

Why Do It?

Although it is certainly en vogue today, it is important to look at why coaches are so keen to adopt it with their teams. Here are just some of the advantages of pressing:

- Keeps opponents from dictating the game
- Stops teams from playing their style
- Makes your players believe they can win
- Encourages your own team and boosts courage
- Keep defenders constantly active and alert
- Makes opposing players do things they don't want to do
- Brings players together because they must count on each other
- Helps weaker players to develop confidence
- Creates cumulative effect on the opposition. Sustained pressing wears them down.
- Strengthens personality and determination
- Allows lesser skilled players to find a role in the team
- Helps counter attacks

Modern Principles of Defending

Both the art and coaching of defending has changed dramatically in recent years. We no longer live in a 'pressure-cover-balance' solution to every attacking problem. Elite forward and midfield players today are being developed to read situations and take advantage at lightning speed. Defensive balance is no longer seen as important a component as it once was. Coaches today like Jurgen Klopp are sacrificing that aspect of the game and defending in an off-balance shape, in return for winning the ball in dangerous areas. Defending in the modern game has now expanded to cover a number of key areas.

✓ *Compactness*
Space is the most important commodity required for teams to attack effectively. Therefore, from a defensive viewpoint, you must reduce space effectively in key areas throughout the game.

✓ *Adaptability*
With detailed scouting systems now implemented at almost every level, the defensive unit will most likely face a different challenge every week. One team may try and exploit space behind, whereas the next week may look at wide areas to attack. Successful defensive systems must be able to cope with different questions every game.

✓ *Discipline*
There are two types of discipline in the game today: mental discipline and physical discipline. Mental discipline is centered around tactics and positioning. Physical discipline is about controlled aggression towards winning the ball and competing. At the top level, a foul is considered a mistake so the best teams must have disciplined players who can consistently perform and make decisions for 90 minutes.

✓ *Communication*

With intricate attacking systems centered around movement and rotation, defenders must give information to their teammates at all times. The volume of a defender usually reveals the intensity in which they play. Effective communication can create role awareness, refocus, build trust, solve problems, and give teams a winning edge.

✓ *Recovery*

The best indicator of a defensively solid team is how quickly they can recover into defensive shape after losing possession. Some of the reasons that teams do not recover defensively include: arguing a ref's decision; assuming a teammate will do it; or not fearing any repercussions from coach or team captain.

Re-Emergence of the Press

In my opinion, there are four reasons why pressing has risen to prominence over the past three years. Firstly, we are potentially coming out of an era where counter attack and controlled football has dominated at the highest level. Yes, the possession game is alive and well, but for every Barcelona and Spain, we have seen defensive units grow stronger, more compact, and consequently, dropping deeper. "Parking the bus" hit the headlines largely because of Jose Mourinho, who showed the world with his Inter Milan and Real Madrid teams that you could frustrate the purists and steal the points. Possession was not required for winning performances and, as a result, big matches on the world stage became a 'cat and mouse' affair with one assuming the aggressor role with the ball and the other looking for the goal on the break. We still have this type of football today with Leicester City remarkably winning the 2016 Premier League, but it is not sustainable, and both fans along with the media want more.

Secondly, pressing is a style of play that the fans can actually relate to. As money and sponsorship have poured into the game and players have become multi-millionaires before they reach 20 years old, the average fan has been somewhat ostracized from the game. Players have become much less accessible, ticket prices have sky rocketed, stadium seating has been redeveloped, and clubs have become global brands. As a result, fans no longer feel connected to their teams like they used to. In addition, as players have become assets and the market has become global, a slow possession game does not excite and engage fans, particularly in the Premier League. English fans want players who will work hard and commit to the club, which pressing certainly does.

Thirdly, as Guardiola brings his style to Germany and Klopp to England, coaches are lifting restrictions they may have previously placed on a style of play due to culture or playing level. As the coaching community, we sometimes look at Barcelona or Atletico Madrid and think that it's a world away from the one in which we work in. The old "but can Messi do it on a cold night in Stoke" argument is still a common school of thought. As top coaches travel however, and take their philosophies with them, we as coaches draw belief that if the system can work across the world and in other words, the belief that this system can work worldwide has risen dramatically. Of course, it helps when they have success with the system and with Guardiola and Klopp competing at the top end of the Premier League table, along with Diego Simeone, Maurizio Sarri, Jorge Sampaoli, and Thomas Tuchel doing the same respectively in their leagues.

Fourthly, as the game has changed over the past twenty years, we have witnessed a dramatic increase in general fitness levels of players. This can be contributed to a number of reasons. The introduction of sports science has educated players and coaches alike on how to prepare, play, and recover in the right way. Players themselves have seen the difference and have bought into this side of the game welcoming new information that comes their way. Coaches are now having more access to players with training times increasing at youth and professional level. We have also seen a change of culture at the professional levels. Football has become a business and the elevation of professional players' financial positions have had to adapt accordingly. The majority of players at the highest level are now looking to maximize their window of potential earnings and have swapped the late nights and alcohol with recovery shakes and sleep pods. All of these changes have had a positive effect on football at professional, youth, and amateur level. As players are maintaining better physical condition, they now have the capacity to work at a higher intensity for longer periods of time and coaches can utilize this by adopting a high tempo system of play.

UEFA Pro License Coach, Liam Bramley, believes that the principles of modern day defending are about denying the opposition:

- Deny the ball

- Deny them time

- Deny the space

- Deny the pass

Hold It Right There…

With the game today attracting worldwide attention and with fans having access to teams 24/7 through social media, it is easy for coaches to get swept up in the pressing craze. Although it brings excitement and the potential rewards are huge, it is an extremely difficult style to implement and the higher the level, the smaller the margin for error is allowed. I believe that most pressing systems fail because teams are not prepared to execute for sustained periods of time and over the course of a game, organization gradually erodes away due to physical and mental fatigue, the emotions of a game, and both collective and individual discipline. Any team can press when the conditions are right and things are going well. It takes a great team, to commit to this standard every single game.

A pressing system is doomed for failure if your team share any of the following characteristics…

- You do not have regular access to players on the training pitch.

- Your team lacks organization and structure.

- Your team lacks speed in crucial areas.

- There is a leadership void on the field with players hesitant to communicate and accept responsibility.

- Your culture is not strong enough and you have players who are unwilling to work hard for each other.

- The climate at which you play is not suited to long periods of high intensity running.

- You have a squad that lacks depth and numbers are a constant issue at training and in games.

- Tactical discipline is a constant problem in your team.

- You approach the game in a relaxed manner on the sidelines and firmly believe that players should have to work out problems and solutions for themselves.

Embrace the Process

There is a school of thought amongst coaches and media that a pressing system is 100% down to the physical qualities of the players. In other words, if you have a group of players with a good physical base (speed, strength, stamina, etc.) and improve their fitness levels, the ability to press effectively should become relatively simple. In some ways you cannot blame people for arriving at that conclusion. At the highest level, the players can make pressing look easy. The coach instructs, the crowd screams, and players seem to respond with passion and drive, and delivers the right amount of work rate to help win the ball back. Sounds pretty straightforward, right? Not quite. One of the aims of this book is to help coaches become aware that pressing is without doubt the toughest defensive system and requires much more than just a physical advantage over the opposition. Pep Guardiola argued that it actually cuts down on running that the players will be required to do. "Pressuring high limits the amount of running players must do. When you win back the ball, there are 30 meters to goal rather than 80".

The ability to effectively implement a pressing system therefore requires a number of conditions. The players must have a profound understanding of the system and what kind of movements they should make at what time. There is an enormous amount of teaching required as this particular philosophy is only as strong as the weakest link. It also takes a complete willingness from every single player and staff to develop and commit to the game plan. Arrigo Sacchi also pointed to the decision making process as key. "Pressing is not about running and it's not about working hard. It's about controlling space"

This is not a book that develops a pressing system into a periodized plan nor looks at managing training loads. Although I fully respect and embrace the role sport science plays in our game, I do not believe there is a fixed template for all teams to follow. What works for Barcelona or Manchester City is not guaranteed to work with your team, unless you play in the Premier League or La Liga. Managing your training load is an important aspect of coaching, but it is important to note that under-training is just as damaging as over-training, and there are more teams who are not successful in pressing because they are not getting enough exposure to high intensity work through their training program. It is up to you to prescribe the right amounts of work and rest to your team, and I advise all coaches to get advice and education in this area. We will focus more closely on training methods and tactical models in this book.

I urge any coach who is considering pressing to immerse yourself and your team in the process of developing the right habits, understanding, and consistency required to excel in this side of the game. We will spend the following 8 chapters looking at how you can do the following:

- Structure a playing model that enables your team to press effectively.
- Examine training exercises that embed pressing into your team's culture and DNA.
- Take a closer look at gegenpressing and how to use it with your team.
- Study how the top coaches approach pressing and set up their systems during games.
- Build a defensive pressing system that can adapt to a variety of tactical situations.
- Consider the role of the coach in helping or hindering a team who want to press at a high level.
- Define ways to measure the effectiveness of your pressing system rather than simply looking at the score line.
- Develop an authentic style of coaching that compliments the style of play you wish to implement with your team.

2

The 'Why' Before the 'How'

"Pep doesn't just give you orders. He also explains why." – Gerard Pique

As we have already identified, in order to press effectively your players must have a firm knowledge of the game and how situations develop throughout it. Although pressing brings initial excitement and huge potential rewards, it is an extremely difficult style to implement and the higher the level, the smaller the margin for error is allowed. I believe that most pressing systems fail because teams are simply not prepared to execute for sustained periods of time, either from fitness levels, focus, or the habits of the players. Any team can press when the conditions are right and things are going well. It takes a great team with a deep understanding to commit to this standard every single game. In this book, we are not going to take any shortcuts and will respect the process of designing an effective template that our players can understand and implement on a consistent basis.

Without an effective way of teaching a defensive system and providing effective information to our players, the vision of a coach will not be strong enough to create the desired behaviours on the field, no matter how passionate they are. This is a crucial starting point in this workbook because coaching today, due to the media in large part, has been caught up in the global sensationalism within the game. With Chelsea pulling away from everyone at the top of the Premier League this season, we are led to believe that Conte's three at the back is the new answer. In the same way, for the past five years 4-4-2 has been depicted as a system that is no longer conducive to the modern game. As coaches, we must rise above these labels and look deeper into the game. The rules of the game may be similar to 20 years ago, but how we understand it, and more importantly teach it, has become much more complex.

"As a coach, you are the 'thinker and leader of the team.' You must have a clear idea of the game and what you want; your clear idea is typically influenced by all your preceding experiences of the game. Training is how you transmit your thinking to your players. They need to understand what you are looking to achieve." (Xavier Tamarit, 'What is Tactical Periodization?')

Establish a Model of Play

"The most important thing in a team is to have a certain model, certain principles, to know them well, to interpret them well, regardless of whether they are used by this or that player." Jose Mourinho

Before we even start to focus on defending, the coach must develop a model of play, which the team will adopt throughout the season. This part of planning is perhaps the most critical step to building a pressing system because it will define exactly what the game will look like (both in and out of possession) and how we need to prepare our players on every level (physical, technical, tactical, and mental). A playing model is similar to a coaching philosophy but is slightly more practical and goes into a little more depth, identifying crucial areas and taking a number of factors into consideration which can impact philosophy. The primary purpose of a playing model is to define exactly what the team intends to become over a period of time. It is neither a set of formations or tactics, but instead contains detailed principles that the team will adopt throughout their training and games. Barcelona coach Luis Enrique believes in the basics when it comes to identifying the playing model; "It's the coach's job to decide his team's style of play, how they attack and how they defend. They have to be effective at both ends of the pitch." Without a plan or model, the team is essentially rudderless, handing over responsibility to luck and excuses.

Playing Model Examples

The idea of a Playing Model was created by Vito Frade, a retired lecturer in Portugal, who developed the concept of Tactical Periodization while writing his dissertation in 1988. In essence, it is the style the coach and players have in mind and want the team to execute in the game itself. It is not aimed at predicting every moment of the game, but instead allows players the opportunity to read and react to key stages together. It can be constructed in a number of different ways and is not exclusively designed for elite and senior level where results and pressure reign. These practices can also be used at the youth level where part of the emphasis is to coach and develop both the team and the individual player. The model on the next page is designed by youth coach, Sam Bensley (@Sambo_bis), who focuses on the development side of coaching. In Sam's model, he identifies the individual goals for each player he has alongside his tactical model. For youth coaches this is very important because you are still teaching the game in essence. The playing model here defines the basics and also educates the players on how to learn systems and critical areas that they will see more of as they develop and get older. Too often development is regarded as skill and technical qualities, but more and more players are arriving at a higher level without an understanding of the game. By separating the team and the player, Sam allows young players to become more process orientated and patient in their development. It is a crucial tool to communicate key growth areas with parents and club coaches.

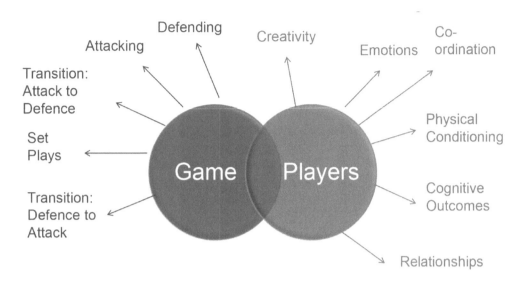

The second example of a playing model is designed by Tim Palmer (@timpalmerftbl) who coaches at St Josephs College in Australia and also works as an analyst for Prozone. Tim works with older players who are now at the stage where results are part of the criteria. He has highlighted similar themes to Sam but has added sub-sections within each area that he also focuses on. As a result, his model is slightly more complex with additional information, both in and out of possession, for his players to interpret and understand. Without having seen his team play, we can tell from his language and terminology that he wants his team to control the game through possession and press high and compact as a unit. Tim is dealing with older players so the terminology can become a little bit more complex, as can the tactical ideas.

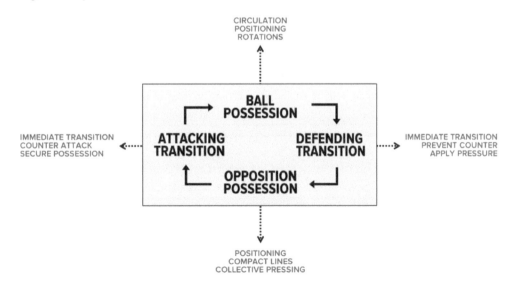

Once the playing model is established, the primary goal of the coaching staff is now how to communicate it effectively to the players. This is such an important process because it clarifies the purpose and direction and allows everyone to see the aims and objectives of your system. It tells everyone where you are going and gives you a map. It also acts as a foundation from which all training and conversations on the field should be derived. Below are a number of reasons adapted from 'Modern Soccer Coach: Pre-Season Training', as to why a playing model is important to have before the season starts.

Flexibility - A playing model is much stronger than a formation, primarily because of its flexibility. A coach can still apply the same principles from the playing model but use a different formation. The best example of this is Pep Guardiola who has used dozens of formations at Bayern Munich during his three years there but his principles have remained consistent. Set formations can change based on the opponent or the score, so they are not a strong enough foundation from which to build.

Removes Panic – If results don't go your way when the games start up, the last thing you want to be doing as a coach is questioning fitness levels, team selection, refereeing decisions, or all three of these. With an effective playing model established, coaches can see what is not working or needs improvement and then prioritize their work. It allows coaches to remain calm while they plan their work and then work their plan.

Enhances Communication – Nothing frustrates players more than mixed messages from the coaching staff which results in confusion over assumed roles and responsibilities. The playing model gives the players and coaching staff a common ground from which they can discuss a variety of different themes. The more soccer-based conversations that can happen within a program, the better off the team will be as relationships are built and strengthened on regular interaction.

Set Specific Objectives for Players – Good coaching requires setting specific goals and standards, and then managing them throughout the season. Many players have one preseason goal: to establish a starting place in the team. By creating and working alongside a playing model, the staff is now challenging the players in a couple of different ways. It's not about beating out Player X to the positon, it's about understanding the position and helping the team becoming successful. The playing model is also designed to enhance the quality and quantity of feedback.

Gives Team Purpose and Direction – To be successful in the long-term, a team requires an identity beyond simply trying to win games. The stronger the identity, the more the players are willing to put into the team, both on and off the field. Focusing frantically on what matters most daily energizes a team and energy is gold dust during preseason and beyond.

Empowers the Players – The best way to maximize players' energy and focus levels is to give them co-ownership of their journey. Once players have a responsibility to the team, great things begin to happen and they will commit even more energy and commitment to the cause. Accountability soon becomes second nature and no player wants to let down their team.

Influence Planning of Training Content – Once the playing model is established, it will drive the session planning and make it much easier to prioritize work. In the book 'Pep Confidential', Guardiola's assistant coach, Lorenzo Buenaventura, commented on the consistency between

Guardiola's model and his training methodology. "Each exercise incorporates an aspect of Pep's football philosophy."

How to Develop a Model of Play

"Every game action, regardless of the four moments of the game in which it might happen, involves a decision (tactical dimension), an action or motor skill (technical dimension) that required a particular movement (physiological dimension) and is directed by volitional and emotional states (psychological dimension)." (Oliveira, 2004)

Although organized and practiced in great detail, because of the nature of the game a playing model cannot be completely rigid. There must be a certain level of flexibility based on the situations that can occur and will occur over the course of a season. It also takes time to develop a model and must take a number of factors into consideration. Below are seven ways that it can be built and developed by the coaching staff.

1. **Identify the strengths of your team.** The model should be built with the players in mind. That must be the starting point. The players should be evaluated on every level (technical, physical, tactical, and mental) before deciding on what areas to prioritize.
2. **Stick to Your Beliefs** – A playing model must also be consistent with the principles of the game which the coach values most highly. These can change from coach to coach and can be somewhat unique. The beautiful thing about the game is that we all interpret it in a slightly different way so this is the coaches' opportunity to put their own spin on their work.
3. **Create a Common Language** – Although the team can all speak the same language; the coach can sometimes use a dialogue which the players do not understand. All staff and players should be aware and use the same terminology and understand the correct context in which it is used.
4. **Keep It Simple** – The idea is not to confuse the players, nor highlight the knowledge of the coach. The more complex your views on the game are, the more you should break it into pieces for the players so they can digest the information more easily. Simple is harder than complex and successful coaches are very good at breaking the game down to help players understand information and apply it to their game.
5. **Be Realistic** – We all want to play like Barcelona but the reality is that most of us are not fortunate to play at the Nou Camp every other week. Your playing model instead must be consistent with the playing styles and abilities of your players. When developing his own model, Jose Mourinho said, "You can't create a contradiction with the idea you want for the game. If your team does not play from the back in a game, do not incorporate this in your exercises."
6. **Share It** – We have already mentioned that the playing model must be clear in the minds of the coaching staff, let's not forget that the players are the most important recipients of it. If they consistently hear messages relating back to it, the chances of them embracing and understanding it, increase drastically. When players are mindful of the process that drives results, teams begin to intentionally improve.
7. **Stick with It** – Having a playing model does not guarantee success but working hard at it over a long period of time does give you a great opportunity. Even after a defeat, it is important that the coaching staff review and understand that this is a process and that will help grow through time, and most importantly, quality work. It's not enough for players to understand a system of play. They must buy into in and have belief that they can master it and perform it under pressure.

Aligning Your Playing Model to Pressing

"Do you know how Barca won the ball back so much? They never had to run back more than 10m due to their positioning." Johan Cruyff

Ultimately, how your team acts and behaves when they are in possession of the ball will play a crucial role in how successful you can be without it. For example, if a team plays an expansive game with a lot of spacing in terms of width and depth, they will struggle to high press immediately because the distances are too great. Likewise, if a team is unbalanced and overloads attackers in a certain area, they too will struggle when possession is lost as their opponent will eventually exploit those spaces. It is therefore vital that a coach looks closely at their attacking organization and studies how it can influence defensive shape and transitions. Below are a number of characteristics in possession that the great pressing teams have shared.

- ✓ **Short Passes** – If you want to have prolonged periods of pressing, you must have a team that excels in short passing. Pep Guardiola wants his team to complete at least 15 passes in the build-up phase in order to destabilize the opposition *and* have numbers around the ball to provide numerical superiority in and out of possession.
- ✓ **Key Relationships** – Players must understand one another's game and be comfortable playing together if you want possession to be a key focal point. They will then have a better chance of anticipating movements, increasing passing possibilities, and working hard for each other if possession does break down.
- ✓ **Possession with Progression** – If you want to press the ball high up the field, you must get your team to 'push up' as a compact unit when they are in possession of the ball. Possession across the back four must therefore move the defensive line higher up the field. This allows players to already be in pressing positions if or when possession is lost.
- ✓ **Patient Build-Up** – If the possession is fast and direct, the ball is always going right back to the opposition and it is almost impossible to sustain a pressing system for long periods of time. Of course, slower possession invites pressure from the opposition, but it also allows the team to move up together.
- ✓ **Positional Balance** – This is where tactical discipline becomes key in the defensive. Players who drift, either by accident or design, can cause problems in defensive transitions if there are no players occupying an area that the opposition can exploit immediately. Tactical fluidity is welcomed in possession, but only if the players who change possession can perform the new function defensively.
- ✓ **Concentration** – This is a very underrated aspect of possession. We tend to look at concentration and focus as defensive qualities or during a moment of transition, but in the build-up phase, your team must be aware of individual and team movement patterns so that they can move the opposition accordingly and react quickly in transition.
- ✓ **Role of a Goalkeeper** - When a defensive line pushes up the pitch, it is critical to have a goalkeeper who is comfortable playing off their line. Manuel Neuer has almost redefined the starting point of attacks and 1v1s because of his willingness to become an extra outfield player. In possession, a goalkeeper with the ability to receive from both sides, read pressure, and with an excellent range of passing, can help a team immensely in the build-up phase.
- ✓ **Dominate Central Areas** – The majority of teams today are using employing three central midfielders to gain control of center of the pitch. Even 4-4-2 systems now are either organized as a diamond or with one of the center forwards dropping off when their

team is not in possession of the ball. Even in a fluid system, every good possession based team today will have two players in the central zone at all times.

✓ **Distance between front and back.** When you blend forwards who stay high up the field with defenders who are slow to push up together, you create a situation that makes it almost impossible to high or medium press. It also creates a vacuum for midfield players to cover that will make it very difficult for them on the defensive side of the ball.

Defensive Organization

"If you have good players, they know how to regain the ball before they lose possession."
Erik Hamren

In creating and developing your play model, you must identify the behaviors you would like your team to assume when they do not have the ball. In communicating this with the team, it is critical that all players understand their roles, responsibilities and purpose during each phase of the game. As we identified in Chapter One, there are three types of pressing when it comes to defensive organization.

High Press – The defensive team moves high up the pitch to apply pressure in the opponent's half with the goal of winning the ball back or forcing the opponent to make a mistake.

Medium Block – A balanced system where pressure is applied in both the team's and opponent's halves. The defensive team is neither pushing up aggressively nor sitting deep.

Low Block – A team drops into its own half to defend, with the 18-yard box typically as a reference point for the defensive line. The prevention of goal scoring opportunities in the final third is the primary goal.

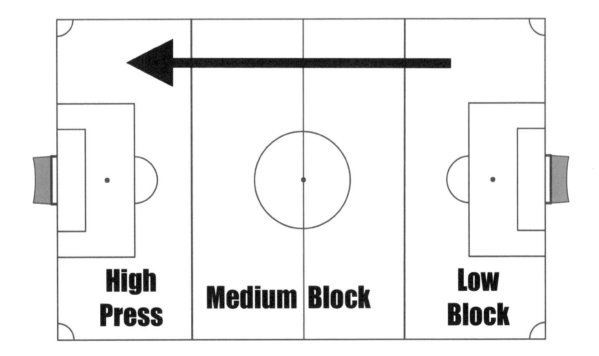

Low Block, Medium Block or High Press?

Why Play a High Press?

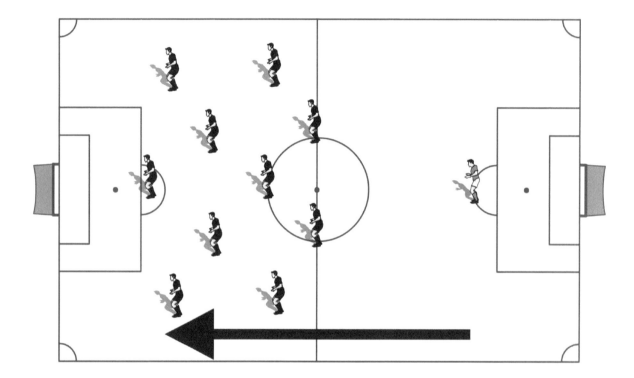

- The rewards of being close to opposition goal and playing against a disorganized defensive unit cannot be understated. In the modern game, pressing has become a form of playmaking. Michael Caley's studies in the Premier League from 2012-2014 showed that a successful tackle in the central area of the field, up to 40 to 50 yards from goal, resulted in a shot twice out of ten times. In comparison, approximately only 2% of attacking moves lead to shots. This shows exactly how rewarding it can be to win the ball high up the field, even against elite opposition.

- It gives you an opportunity to win back possession immediately after losing it.

- It can remove pressure for your back four to essentially do all the defending. When every player has a responsibility to press and win possession, it creates a collective defensive mentality.

- It stops the opposition from constructing their attack and building momentum. If you are playing against a possession based team, this is usually where they draw their confidence from.

- The majority of teams are reluctant to build out when any pressure is applied so you can force the opposition to go long into an area where you should have a numerical advantage.

Why Play a Medium Block?

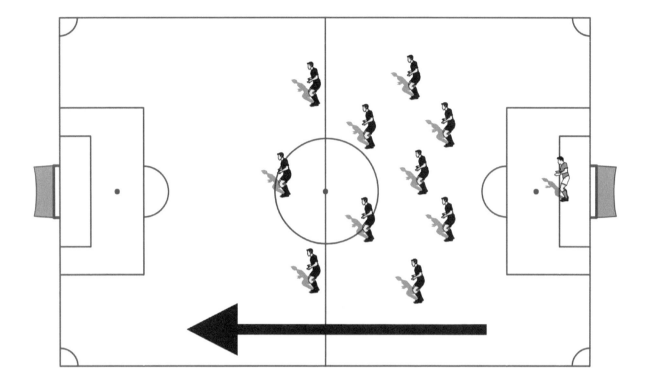

- It is a lot easier to organize your team with clear reference points (e.g. center circle) which allows the team to create a cohesive block and in doing so, significantly reduces the initial decision making process for each individual.

- If the opponent is in possession and the distances are too great, your team is unbalanced, or there is simply no access to the ball, your team will be exposed if they attempt to press. It is therefore better to drop, re-organize and attempt to find a new opportunity to win back possession.

- By allowing your team to recover and drop deeper, it makes it difficult for the opposition to play through and forces them to either play over or around the medium block, two much more difficult ways to attack.

- A medium block creates a numerical superiority in a central area and prevents penetration. It is also difficult for attacking players to receive the ball in areas in which they can turn and create.

- It protects your defenders from penetration through midfield and forces the opponent to pass sideways or backwards.

- It is much less demanding on your players both physically and mentally. If players have not become conditioned to press or are playing against a team who excels in possession, it can help the players pick and choose their moments of applying pressure.

- It allows you to create more pressing traps once the team is in good shape. We will look closer at pressing triggers in Chapter 6.

Why Play a Low Block?

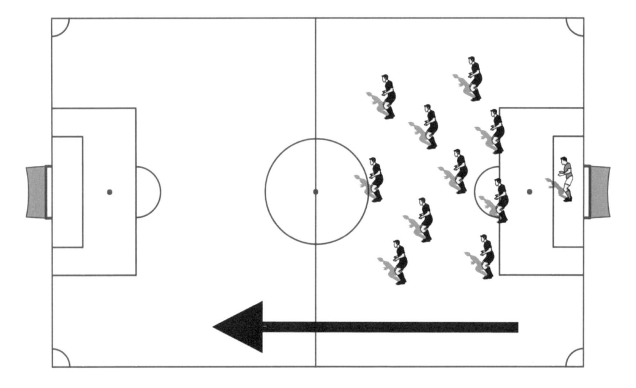

- It makes play very compact with minimal space and is difficult for the attacking team to break you down.

- If you are playing against a direct team who do not intend to use possession in their build-up, a low block can allow you to get initial position quickly and then have players around the ball who can help compete for it after it is delivered.

- It allows defenders to read the game easier as the pitch becomes smaller and also puts them in a position where they can intercept passes and be more aggressive because of increased defensive support.

- There will be a number of opportunities to counter attack when the ball is won with plenty of space behind the opposition defensive line.

- It pushes opponents wide where they may have limited options and then allows you to provide defensive cover quickly.

You Might Need All Three!

Of course, the game quickly teaches us that there is not one solution to every problem. Throughout the season, there will be a number of challenges for coaches and their defensive systems, so becoming adaptable is very important. At the majority of levels, it is almost impossible to press aggressively for 90 minutes. There are stages of a match where players need to recover and regain control of the game. Below are factors that may cause you to change your defensive organization before or during the game.

- **Condition of Your Players**
  - Fitness levels
  - Speed in key areas
  - Ability to make quick decisions

- **Game Management**
  - Score
  - Time remaining

- **Number of Players Available**
  - Substitutes
  - Red cards
  - Injuries

- **Pitch Conditions**
  - Size of field
  - Poor surface

- **Quality of Opposition**
  - Ability to play against press
  - Direct or indirect
  - Danger players

- **Tournament Play**
  - Increased number of games
  - Limited rest
  - Emotional component

- **Development Level**
  - Teach players different systems
  - Challenge players to solve problems
  - Lessons in defeat

Even at the highest level, a change in defensive system can happen without prior planning from the coach. When Liverpool defeated Manchester City 1-0 on December 31st 2016, Jurgen Klopp received immediate praise for his approach to the game from the television pundits. Although almost everyone expected Liverpool to come out with their traditional high press, they predominately used a medium block to contain Manchester City and limit their space to create. However, when Klopp was asked about his master stroke after the game, he revealed that was not how he had specifically prepared his team. "It's not that we had a clear plan from the first second to stay deeper than we do in other games, but you have to learn and adapt during the game. You have to take the shape you have and then try to score and win the game. We knew that we needed to be compact tonight, wherever we defend." Although Klopp has the luxury of working with elite players who can make adjustments during the game, his message is an important one. Sometimes the quality of your opponents will cause the game to change and you must be flexible enough to put your team in a position to win the game. Of course, it is easier for a team conditioned in high pressing to drop than it would be for a low-block team to adjust and begin to press, but knowing when to do it and having everyone on the same page is vital for success.

Get Defensive Transitions Right!

Once the organization of the team is established, both in and out of possession, transitions then become crucial to the success of the play model. As a coach, of course, you want the opposition to play against your organized defensive system as much as possible. Therefore, when the ball is lost your team must be conditioned to react quickly and effectively. With the counter attack being such a prominent part of the modern game, teams must now be equipped to prevent it. The first goal therefore, is for your team to quickly reorganize themselves and close gaps so that the opposition cannot take advantage of spaces. Elite teams excel in transitional moments by creating various lines to support one another.

"The longer we have the ball, the less can happen against you. Then you lose it and you need to get it back, I thought it's a good idea to get it back immediately, because it makes life easier." Jurgen Klopp

When structuring your playing model for this phase, it is important that players know the answers to the following questions during transitions:

- Can we press? Do players have access to the ball?

- When do you want your players to press?

- Where on the pitch do you want to press?

- For how long are your players expected to press the ball?

- Should we show opponents inside or outside?

"Many teams also have problems deciding when to stop pressing, i.e. when do you stop pressing if you can't win the ball back? When should you retreat? How long should you press and with how many players? This is particularly problematic because the position of the ball is always changing. Immediately after losing the ball the team should press at top speed and with maximum intensity for five seconds." – Rene Maric

The attitude of players must stay or become aggressive, as your team changes from attack-minded to defensive-minded. Barcelona famously used the '5 Second Rule' under Guardiola where they aggressively pressed for five seconds before retreating and re-organizing if they failed to win possession. That time frame has almost become an unwritten guideline at the elite level, where only ultra-aggressive pressing teams attempt to sustain their initial counter press for any longer. If you cannot win possession back right away, players do not necessarily 'give up' defensively, but rather adjust to another style e.g. forcing the opposition wide and use the touchline as a trap or an aid to win the ball back. In my opinion, the most important aspect in Defensive Transitions is 1v1 defending. Every player on your team must not only embrace a defensive mentality, but they must also be proficient at it. If they are beaten easily or quickly, the whole structure of the team is compromised.

Below are four basic keys to defensive transitions that I have used with my teams:

✓ Positive reaction of player who just lost the ball

✓ Prevent penetration either by dribbling or forward passes

✓ Overload shape on the ball side to provide cover and numerical superiority

✓ Communicate in order to get everyone moving and working together

Summary

✓ As coaches, we are sometimes guilty of complicating the game for our players, but it basically boils down to what you do when you have possession and how you react when you do not.

✓ A team cannot choose to adopt a pressing style and expect to be successful without the coach first developing a global picture of how the team will play in and out of possession.

✓ The system is based on the strengths and weaknesses of the specific players on the team. You cannot take another model and attempt to directly apply it to your team.

✓ The physical demands are so high and complex that players are not naturally conditioned to sustain an effective pressing style for 90 minutes after one or two training sessions or without maximizing time during pre-season.

✓ If a coach decides to implement a pressing system midway through the season, the players have been conditioned to work with entirely different intensity levels and will have to be re-trained to perform at the required level. This could take weeks and could risk injuries because of the increased training load alongside a regular game schedule.

✓ A pressing style of play must be developed early and the specificity of training will play a huge part in the success or failure. Time on task is needed to teach and coach key aspects such as angles, cues, shape, triggers, and traps. It takes the same commitment to learning the system as it does to winning the ball back.

✓ Concentration and focus in transitions must be trained and worked on alongside your specific offensive and defensive shape.

✓ Successful defensive teams are quicker at finding solutions, adjusting their shape, and anticipating the situations that will develop based on the flow of the game. This is a teachable skill.

3
Pressing Player Profiles

A pressing system is only as strong as its weakest link. Your team may be almost perfect in their shape and organization, but if one player does not fulfil their role, the defensive shape will be exposed. Of course, not every player can do it. Some lack the required speed or endurance which makes pressing almost impossible, especially against quality opposition. Others have spent so long working in a training environment that is based predominately on small sided games that they are conditioned to run shorter distances and lack the capacity for continuous higher intensity runs. We all know that high fitness levels are required to press, and those requirements will increase in elite competition. Some teams use Strength and Conditioning or Sports Science staff to help them in this area, and the physical demands will change depending on the level.

It is important to be aware, however, that not every limitation is physical. Think about the fast, athletic player who can run and close down opposing players at full speed, only to watch the left back stroll past them as they make a half-hearted attempt at a challenge. Or the forward who loses focus at the vital moment of transition and fails to apply pressure quick enough, allowing the center back enough time to pick a pass and find a teammate. It is also quite common to have players whose work ethic and decision making ability fails to match their athleticism, resulting in a reluctance to accept a role in a pressing system.

Liverpool defensive work comparison

Player	Min per tackle/intercept	Player	Min per recovery
Philippe Coutinho	35	Sadio Mane	15
Adam Lallana	37	Philippe Coutinho	15
Roberto Firmino	37	Adam Lallana	18
Sadio Mane	45	Roberto Firmino	27
Daniel Sturridge	**348**	**Daniel Sturridge**	**87**

Above is an analysis of the Liverpool forward line by Sky Sports and Adam Bate in October 2016. Daniel Sturridge is a perfect example of how we need to look deeper than speed and fitness levels when we are constructing and managing our pressing systems. At full fitness, Sturridge ticks every physical box in the game. He has the explosiveness, speed, and athleticism to outrun the majority of defenders in the Premier League. Jurgen Klopp, however, has been reluctant to use Sturridge at key stages during the first half of the season, even when fully fit. His defensive statistics (above) show us why this may be. Sturridge clearly does not show the same enthusiasm towards the defensive side of the game as he does when the ball is at his feet. Klopp himself hinted at Sturridge's journey in the game as a reason for his reluctance. "It is not easy. Most of his life, football has been so easy because he is so skilled. I think this is a very useful moment in his career." Attitude and willingness to work play such a big role in applying this kind of defensive system, and we will talk in Chapter 9 about how we can positively affect work ethic as coaches.

Without question, speed is a major component to pressing, but we must look deeper as we work with our players. Jorge Valdano argues there are three types of speed in his book, 'The Infinite Game' which are impacted by personality, technical ability and intelligence levels.

- ✓ Speed by running – movement in a certain distance
- ✓ Speed by thinking – ability to make split second decisions
- ✓ Speed by technique – speed of play and precision of technique

Therefore, without the ability to make the correct decisions, execute defensive actions under pressure, and embrace the system, players with speed and aggression, are not guaranteed to be successful in a pressing game. The higher the level, the more intelligence is required from the pressing team and the greater the consequences are if they get it wrong. I believe that this aspect of pressing is overlooked by a lot of coaches and we tend to generalize our players as having great 'game intelligence' or lacking it. Instead, it is a complex awareness, focus, and identifying triggers – all of which can be coached. Before deciding to press, each player must make the following decisions:

- Which player do I leave in order to go and press?
- What angle do I approach from?
- What is the risk-reward of going to press?
- Where do I recover to after pressing?

Methodology Matters

"A mental landscape must be created because the development of a game must be born in the head of the players first." Vitor Frade

Our goal with this workbook is to attempt to connect the technical, physical, tactical and mental components required to play a pressing game and maximize individual and collective output. Therefore, the structure of our training program and exercises we use with our team are both critical in coaching an effective pressing system. Traditional 2v2 exercises like the one below have been used by a number of coaches for years when it comes to coaching individual and principles of defending. It is a good coaching tool for young players at the early stage of their development, but when it comes to coaching an aggressive, defensive system of play, it is somewhat outdated for a number of reasons. Firstly, the players are playing in a small area which decreases the physical demands and makes it easier to defend as time and space are limited for attackers. Secondly, players are constantly performing the same defensive actions over and over again, which virtually eliminates any decision-making component. Thirdly, the exercise is significantly limited by the attacking ability of your players. If you are not fortunate to have an abundance of 1v1 artists, then the defenders may find it quite easy. Fourthly, it only works on defending against a dribble or a combination player (i.e. one-two, give-and-go, or overlap) to beat the pressure. In reality, however, a ten-yard pass and time on the ball does greater damage to any pressing system. Fifthly, and most importantly for me, is that players struggle to connect this situation to the game. As coaches, we can easily see 1v1 and 2v2 situations arise throughout a match, but because the game constantly flows, players themselves fail to make the associations because of additional players and bigger, specific areas of the pitch. Because of these limitations, I would advise coaches to be more specific with their training methods and planning.

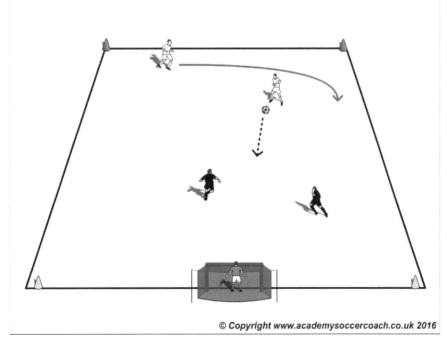

Our tactical, physical, and technical training model must be supported by positional and functional work if our players are to develop and excel tactically. This is not about changing our training program; it's about enhancing it. Remember, players cannot change what they cannot see. If we help them define performance, we are in a great position to help them improve it. Only then will we see our culture improve and have players go the extra yard to get better.

Working with players in a position-specific setting will lead to:

- ✓ More confident players – With specific practice in game-like situations, players will feel better prepared going into games and fully aware that they possess the tools needed to meet any challenges that arise.

- ✓ Better understanding of roles and responsibilities – Players will develop recognition of what is expected of their positions and themselves specifically. They will also gain an appreciation of key relationships within the game (e.g. full back and wide midfielder combining).

- ✓ More accountability – As players understand what is being asked of them within their position and skill level, the coach can now give the player responsibility to perform these tasks.

- ✓ Fewer question marks over performance - With a training model that focuses on the individual as well as the team, the coach will be fully aware of what each player can do. If a player lacks understanding of any aspect of the game, the coach is likely to find this out more quickly in this setting, rather than through traditional trial and error.

- ✓ Embracing Additional Practice – As players see the benefits of specialized training, they will learn effective practice techniques that they can implement on their own or with a teammate.

'How' you train individuals and specific positions also plays an important role in its success. It requires the same amount of planning and energy that goes into team training sessions, and the responsibility is with the coaching staff to create 'buy-in' from the players. Therefore, in order to maximize your positional training, the following principles from 'Modern Soccer Coach: Position-Specific Training' must be taken into consideration:

Define Positional Demands - Coaches must define what they need from each position specific to the level. There may be differences in formations, styles of play, and systems. This is done alongside your Play Model (Chapter Two).

Specificity - Practice the exercise in the exact same area of the field where we want them to happen. In 'What is Tactical Periodisation', Xavier Tamarit argues that it is extremely important to train in the same contexts that players will see in the game. This helps in both decision making and interactions of the team.

Don't Be General - Simply splitting the team into attackers and defenders for the session is not position-specific training. It may be an easy option from an organizational point of view, but it limits the connection between practice and the game which is our primary goal.

Understand Players' Strengths and Weaknesses - This is where you must find balance as a coach. Each player is different.

Game Specific Exercises - As a coach, you must identify exact scenarios that players find themselves in, in a game, and work from there. Coaches must identify specific movements that translate directly to a player's position and work to become more consistently explosive with those movements.

Feedback - Without feedback, the player will not improve. Feedback should be centered around ways to measure performance and effective ways to communicate with the players. If we do not speak the language of the player, we cannot expect them to take in vital information and use it to help their game. We will look at this closer in Chapter 9.

Consistency - Position-specific training must be embedded into the training program rather than presented to the players at random moments throughout the season. If you do not see value in this training as a coach, don't expect the players to embrace it. Be consistent with your planning and the players will, in turn, be consistent with their attitudes and performance.

Individual Coaching Points

In Chapter One, we talked about the 'pressure-cover-balance' principles changing in the modern game. Compactness, adaptability, discipline, communication, and recovery are all critical factors when it comes to preventing the opposition from constructing their attacks. Individually and positionally, the important components have also extended to pressure, delay, depth and balance. Below are the key points for each one.

Pressure and Delay - First Defender:

1. Get there quick!
2. Close distance so that the player in possession cannot lift their head and see options
3. Deny forward pass
4. Slow down the attack
5. Attempt to win ball if there is access to it
6. Make play predictable – show them down one side
7. Be patient – do overcommit and get beat easily

Depth - Second Defender:

1. Support the first defender
2. Cover the space behind first defender – judge appropriate distances based on speed and skill of attacker
3. Read the direction of potential pass from body shape of player in possession
4. Communicate with first defender

Balance - Rest of the Team:

1. Pick up any other attackers who may get the ball
2. Cut out passing lanes
3. Be aware of attacking players moving into space in forward positions
4. Be ready to assume role of first or second defender as the play progresses

High Pressing Player Characteristics

Creating a high pressing system invariably involves changing how players think and work, moving away from passive pressure and instead towards aggression with intensity. Now, both hard and smart work play a huge role in improving and sustaining performance levels. Like any change, there will be some uncertainty and fear of the unknown, but if the player has a genuine desire to improve and reach another level, these challenges will be overcome. We must make full use of our influential role as coaches to help players realize how difficult this road will be and what setbacks are coming their way. The next step is to look at how we will implement this program within the different positions of the game. The more specific we can be with our work, the better. It is therefore important to create a player profile for what you are looking for in your defensive system. Some of these points are in possession because of the offensive transition.

Goalkeeper

Tactical

- ✓ Awareness to control the tempo of the game
- ✓ Understanding of when to step and when to drop
- ✓ Ability to 'read' the game and anticipate movement from opposition forward lines

Technical

- ✓ Range of passing – short and long
- ✓ Speed of play and skill to keep the ball moving
- ✓ Ability to receive from one direction and play the other way

Physical

- ✓ Speed over short and long distances
- ✓ Mental and physical endurance to sustain concentration levels
- ✓ Quick reactions so that they can help the team in transitions

Mental

- ✓ Decision making
- ✓ Disciplined
- ✓ Ability to communicate and give constant information to teammates
- ✓ Excellent relationships with defensive unit to pass on and receive information

---

Central Defender

Tactical

- ✓ Awareness of overloads as they occur in defensive areas
- ✓ Comfortable defending spaces in wide areas
- ✓ Understanding of when to step and when to drop
- ✓ Ability to 'read' the game and anticipate movement from opposition forward lines

Technical

- ✓ Range of passing – short and long
- ✓ Angles of support to defenders and midfielders
- ✓ Comfortable defending without immediate cover
- ✓ Solid in 1v1 and 1v2 situations

Physical

- ✓ Speed over short and long distances
- ✓ Ability to turn and change directions
- ✓ Endurance levels
- ✓ Can recover quickly

Mental

- ✓ Leader and organizer of defensive line
- ✓ Accept responsibility when setbacks occur
- ✓ Disciplined
- ✓ Adapt easily to the demands of the game

Full Back

Tactical

- ✓ Constantly provide cover
- ✓ Understanding of distances – when to shift and drop
- ✓ Decision making when to press high
- ✓ Offer width in support during transitions

Technical

- ✓ Defensively strong in 1v1 situations
- ✓ Receive the ball under pressure
- ✓ Ability in the air to defend the back post
- ✓ Stop crosses and block shots

Physical

- ✓ High intensity runs repeatedly
- ✓ Speed to pressure players on their first touch
- ✓ High levels of aerobic and anaerobic endurance
- ✓ Can recover quickly

Mental

- ✓ High concentration levels
- ✓ Ability to make quick decisions
- ✓ Competitive nature
- ✓ High levels of communication

Holding Midfielder

Tactical

- ✓ Disciplined in holding position
- ✓ Ability to 'screen' center backs
- ✓ Slow down counter attacks
- ✓ Position to receive in transition

Physical

- ✓ Speed over short distances
- ✓ High aerobic and anaerobic capacity
- ✓ Speed and change direction in small areas

Technical

- ✓ Range of passing – short and long
- ✓ Capable of defending in 1v1 situations
- ✓ Compete in the air
- ✓ Angles of support, both offensively and defensively

Mental

- ✓ Quick reactions when possession is lost
- ✓ Awareness to track runners
- ✓ Decision making ability, on and off the ball
- ✓ Effective communication and leadership skills

Attacking Midfielder

Tactical

- ✓ Decision making – when to press?
- ✓ Ability to apply aggressive pressure
- ✓ Discipline
- ✓ Understanding of teammates' roles and responsibilities

Physical

- ✓ Acceleration and speed
- ✓ Recover quickly when possession is lost
- ✓ Strength in tackles and pressing
- ✓ High aerobic and anaerobic capacity

Technical

- ✓ Discipline – press without fouling
- ✓ Protect the ball under pressure
- ✓ Create space in transition
- ✓ Penetration in possession – pass or dribble

Mental

- ✓ Team player – willing to work for other players
- ✓ Not afraid to take risks
- ✓ Handles pressure well – always wants the ball
- ✓ Winning mentality – wants to win the ball back quickly!

Wide Attacker

Tactical

- ✓ Strong relationship with full back
- ✓ Recognition of triggers to press
- ✓ Change positions in relation to flow of game
- ✓ Movement in relation to team – stepping and shifting

Technical

- ✓ Excels in basics – passing and receiving
- ✓ Ability to defend in 1v1 and 1v2 situations
- ✓ Dribble and penetrate in offensive transition
- ✓ Understanding to show players inside or outside

Physical

- ✓ Acceleration and speed
- ✓ Ability to recover quickly
- ✓ Aggressive when defending 1v1
- ✓ High aerobic and anaerobic capacity

Mental

- ✓ Embraces high workload off the ball
- ✓ Strong relationship with full back
- ✓ Composure to keep possession in transition
- ✓ Risk taker in possession

Center Forward

Tactical

- ✓ Understanding of team shape and roles
- ✓ Decision making – when to press?
- ✓ Intelligence to 'show' defenders into areas
- ✓ Appreciation of distances of teammates

Technical

- ✓ Discipline – press without fouling
- ✓ Turn a 1v2 situation into a 1v1
- ✓ Take advantage of defensive mistakes
- ✓ Penetration in possession – pass or dribble

Physical

- ✓ Change of speed and direction
- ✓ Aggressive in defensive situations
- ✓ Ability to take physical contact
- ✓ Combination of high aerobic and anaerobic capacities

Mental

- ✓ Willingness to work for the team
- ✓ Leadership role as first line of defense
- ✓ Anticipate defensive actions in possession
- ✓ Determination to compete and harass defenders

Exercise One

Positional Focus: Goalkeepers in the possession and transition phase.

Set-Up: The exercise takes place in a 15x10 yard area, around the six-yard box. There are six players involved, including one goalkeeper. Coach will need a supply of balls for quick restarts and to challenge the goalkeeper's speed of play.

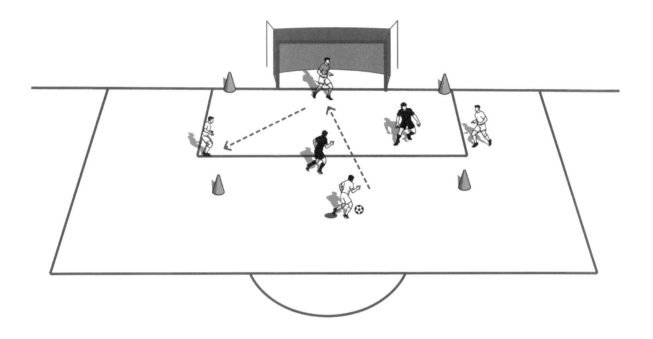

Session Details:

Four players, including the goalkeeper, begin the exercise as the possession team (in white) and take up positions on the outside of the grid. Two players on the inside are the defensive players. It starts as a 4v2 possession game with the team in possession attempting to score with ten consecutive passes or by splitting the two defensive players with one pass. If the defensive players win the ball, they can transition into attack and score immediately in the goal. This will challenge the goalkeeper not only to play quickly in possession, but also to react quickly and make saves when called into action if the defensive pair win the ball. The exercise will last two minutes and then the defensive players will rotate with two players in the possession team. Every player (apart from the goalkeeper) should get at least two sets as a defender.

Progression:

- ✓ Restrict the players on the outside to one touch.

- ✓ Allow the players on the outside to transition defensively inside the area if they lose the ball.

- ✓ If the ball goes outside the area for any reason, the coach will trigger another ball into one of the defensive players to shoot on goal. Again, the players on the outside must react quickly to this scenario and work aggressively to block shots and help the goalkeeper.

- ✓ Make the area bigger and add two players to the exercise. One will work as a defender, while another joins the attacking team as a 'pivot-player' in the middle. The possession team scores a point with ten consecutive passes, and/or if the 'pivot-player' can receive the ball and transfer it to another player on the outside. The same transition rules apply if the three defensive players win the ball. (See below)

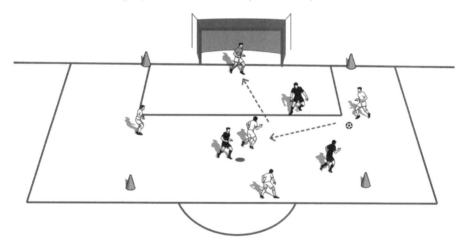

© Copyright www.academysoccercoach.co.uk 2016

Coaching Points:

- ✓ The goalkeeper should be challenged both in and out of possession. Depending on the level, they may struggle technically or in the transition phase.

- ✓ Although the focus of the exercise is on the goalkeeper, it is important that pressing principles are reinforced in other areas too. The game punishes defensive pairs who leave spaces and do not provide cover. They should continually be working and communicating to make sure that this does not happen.

- ✓ Even in the possession group, do not allow players to stand still and remain static. They should be moving up and down the line to offer an option to the player in possession and focusing on how they can help the team. The more energy they show when they have the ball, the higher the chances are that they will react quickly when they ball transitions to the other team.

Exercise Two

Positional Focus: Midfield or defenders. Positional groups where pressure and cover are key principles to prevent penetration on the dribble rather than passes.

Set-Up: The exercise takes place in a 30x30 yard area. Nine players are split into three teams of three players: defensive group, Group 1 and Group 2. Coach will need a supply of balls on the outsides for teams to be ready for quick restarts and to keep intensity levels as high as possible.

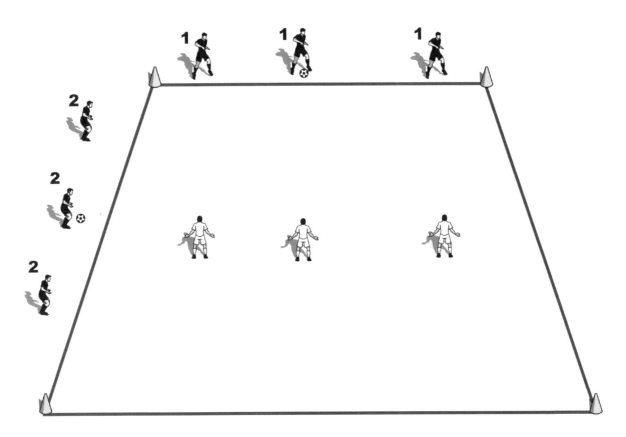

© Copyright www.academysoccercoach.co.uk 2016

Session Details:

The defensive team (white) start in the middle, the teams 1 and 2 on the outside. The coach randomly calls out either Team 1 or Team 2 to start the exercise. If that group is called, a 3v3 game starts against the white team with the objective of the possession team to dribble across the opposite line with the ball under control. Team 1 are attacking from north to south and vice versa, while Team 2 are attacking from east to west and vice versa. The offside rule does apply so the defensive team can find success if they are organized.

The coach will then call another number and the defensive team must continually react and re-organize in relation to where the ball starts. After two minutes, change the defensive team and keep score to see what group had the most success defensively. Continue this rotation for three sets.

Progression:

✓ Change the dimensions on the field to make it even longer or wider.

✓ Remove the offside rule so that now attackers can run beyond the defensive line. How does the defensive team react and solve this problem?

Coaching Points:

✓ The first step for the defensive team is to apply pressure on the ball. This must be done immediately.

✓ Provide cover at all times to the strong side defender.

✓ Once the central player in possession passes to a wide player, the defensive team must create a strong side and keep the attack there.

✓ Once the attack slows down, look for opportunities to double-up and win possession.

Exercise Three

Positional Focus: Wide midfielders in a medium block or the set-up can be adapted and moved higher up the pitch to focus on wide forwards in a high press

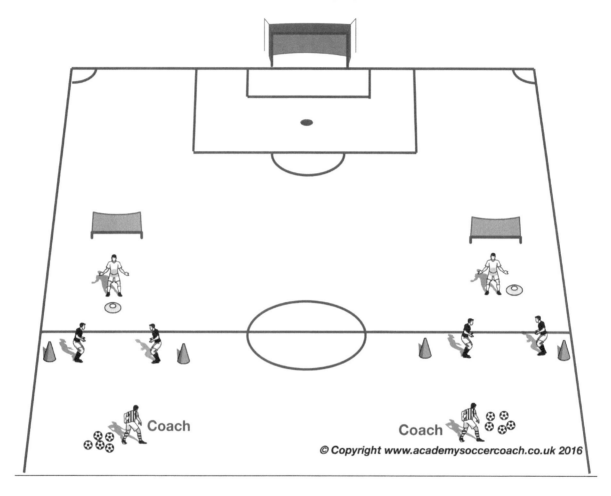

Set-Up:

This is an exercise from Marcelo Bielsa and works on defending against a wall pass and defending 1v1 when the ball is played behind the midfielder. Two sides of the full field are used along with two mini-goals and a supply of balls. Both sides of the field work simultaneously so it is helpful to have a coach on either side to control the speed and provide feedback.

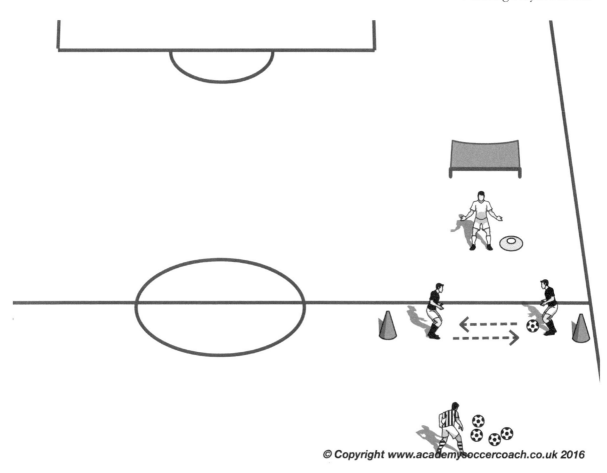

Session Details:

Players work in groups of three. The player in white is the defender (wide midfielder) and the players in black are attackers. The exercise starts with the two attacking players passing the ball back and forth as the defender looks on. On the coach's signal (when the ball is on its way), the defender sprints to the player toward whom the ball is moving. When the ball arrives, the attacking player passes it back and then sprints for a return in behind the defender. The objective for the attacking player is to receive the return and score a goal, while the goal for the defender is to track the run and win the ball back or simply prevent the run. After five defensive actions, change the wide midfielder (black).

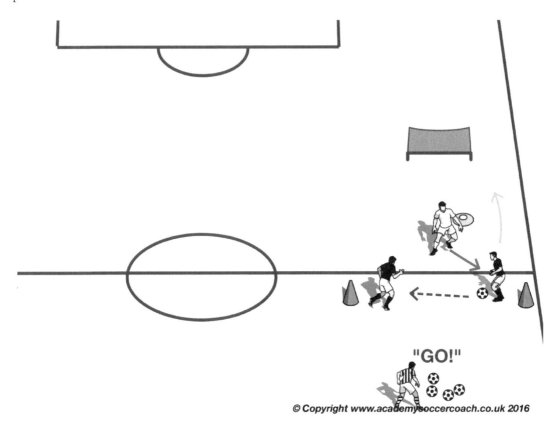

© Copyright www.academysoccercoach.co.uk 2016

Progression:

✓ Move the area further back and work with wide forwards in a high pressing system to do the same functions.

✓ Move the mini-goal further back and now the distances' physical demands are significantly increased.

✓ Add a second ball from the coach after the first ball is gone. The coach can play to the attacker again with a second defensive action for the wide midfielder, or play to the wide midfielder who must dribble forward or find a pass in order to work on offensive transitions.

Coaching Points:

✓ Encourage the defensive player to forward sprint on the initial call. It communicates a pressing action and also will challenge the player to recover quicker, which is what the exercise is about.

✓ As soon as the wide midfielder moves to press and the ball is played square, how quickly can the wide midfielder react and change direction? This will be the key to the defensive phase.

✓ After tracking the run, challenge the defensive player to make physical contact without fouling. This will give the player an idea of the distances required and how important it is to get close at all times.

Exercise Four

Positional Focus: Back four and holding midfielder in a low block.

Set-Up:

This is an exercise from Neil Adair which focuses on a defensive unit working through a variety of different angles and overloads. Four defenders, along with a holding midfielder and a goalkeeper are organized on the white team and take a traditional starting position outside the 18-yard box. The attacking team (in black) have four players who take up central positions, and five others (A-E) who start at fixed points with a supply of balls.

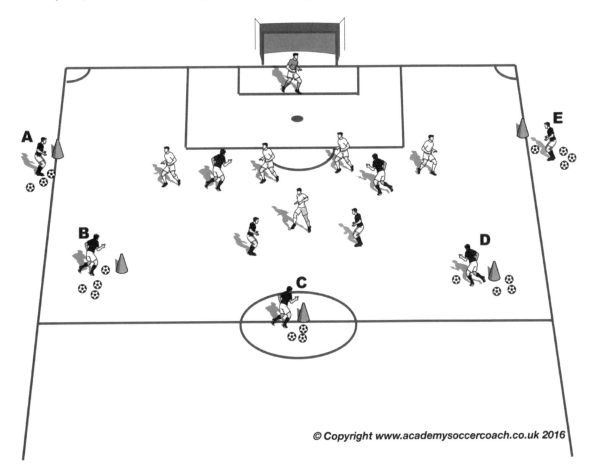

© Copyright www.academysoccercoach.co.uk 2016

Session Details:

Coach triggers the beginning of the exercise by calling out one letter (A-E). The player at that letter then plays a ball forward and creates a 5v5 towards goal. The attacking team have no limitations and the defensive team must simply stop them. The attacking player at A-E has a choice of passing the ball in or dribbling to start the attack. The defensive unit must react accordingly. After the ball is gone, the coach waits ten seconds so that the defensive line can push up, before calling another letter. After 3 minutes rotate the inside attacking players with the outside and play again.

© Copyright www.academysoccercoach.co.uk 2016

Progression:

- ✓ Award the defensive unit a point if they clear the ball or dribble in offensive transition beyond the A-E service line. This should create a competitive element to the exercise which should increase tempo and intensity.
- ✓ Add another forward on the attacking team (black) and organize them into a front three, with two attacking midfielders playing just behind them.
- ✓ Add a defensive midfielder to the white team and now see if they can push their defensive line higher when B, D, or C are in play.

Coaching Points:

- ✓ Organization in relation to the ball is the primary goal of the defensive team. They must get compact and stay connected to one another.
- ✓ Part of the organization phase is applying pressure on the ball. If the defensive line cannot do this, they will never be organized as the attacking team will simply drive forward. Establish whose responsibility it is to apply pressure at each starting point and how the rest of the team should react when this happens.
- ✓ Communication is huge for the defensive team. Every player should be passing on information to each other to keep concentration and aggression levels high.
- ✓ The transition element of the exercise (10 seconds in between attacks) should be used to push the defensive line forward and compact the space. Do not allow defensive players to get drawn towards their own goal during this time.
- ✓ The 5v5 situation is designed to highlight 1v1 defending. Every player on white team must be comfortable in this situation and prevent the ball moving forward with a pass or dribble.

Exercise Five

Positional Focus: Holding midfielders in a medium or low block.

Set-Up:

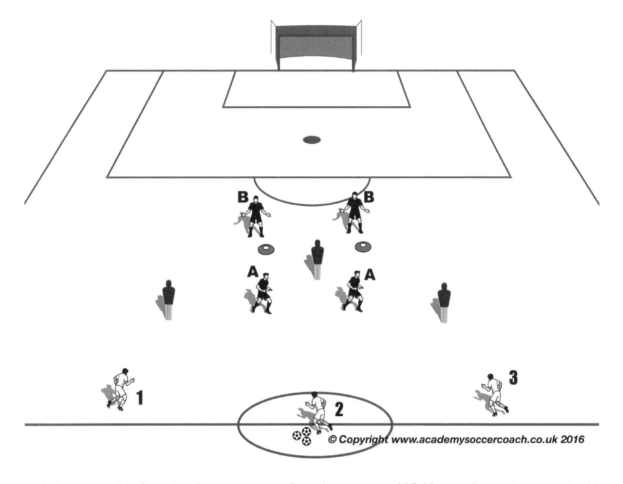

This is an exercise from Louis Lancaster and works on two midfielders acting as 'screeners' with the objective of intercepting forward passes. Two defensive midfielders work at a time (in black) and three attacking players are used continuously. Three mannequins and a supply of balls are required to keep the session flowing.

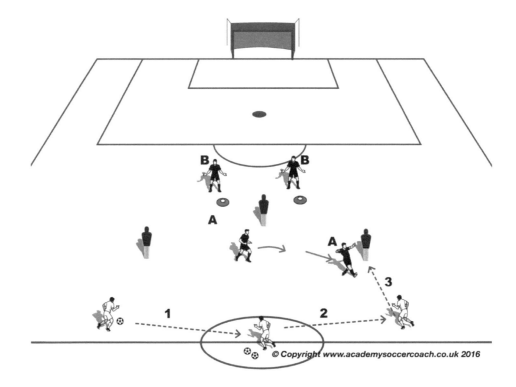

Session Details:

The three players in white start the exercise by passing to each other. The first holding midfield pairing (A's) must move in relation to the ball. The white players are limited to two touches and are looking to hit the mannequin in front of them for a goal. Players 1 and 3 can hit the mannequin in the middle also. The only restriction with their passing patterns is that player 1 cannot pass to player 3 and vice versa. This gives the midfielders the opportunity to continually shift across. The goal of the midfield pairing is to block forward passes towards the mannequin. To be effective, they must work together with one player stepping to the mannequin directly in front, while the other covers the middle mannequin. They then switch roles when the ball is switched across. Players work for three minutes and then defensive pairings switch with B's.

Progression:

- ✓ Move the mannequins further apart to increase the physical demands.
- ✓ Allow the attacking players to dribble and award them an extra point if they beat one of the holding midfielders in a 1v1 situation.

Coaching Points:

- ✓ Defensive angles of support are very important. When one defensive player steps, the other must cover in behind. They should never be flat or square when passes are played forward.
- ✓ The defensive players should 'read' the intentions of the attacking players in order to save them from over committing on either side. Body shape and receiving positions of the attacking players should dictate their intentions for a forward or square pass.
- ✓ When the ball travels, the defensive players must move quickly. There should never be a fixed position in this exercise.

Exercise Six

Positional Focus: Fullbacks in a medium or low block working on a 1v1 and 2v2 situations with a transitional element.

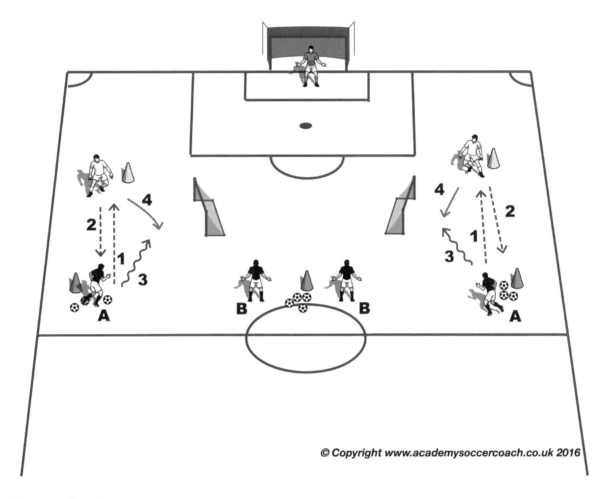

Session Details:

The first part of the exercise is a basic 1v1 with an attacker aiming to drive inside. The exercise begins with the attacker (player A) passing to the defender. Both sides go at the same time. As the defender plays the ball back to player A, it turns into a 1v1 situation with the attacker looking to score in the mini-goal. The attacker has 6 seconds to score. As soon as that time has expired, the two central attackers (B players) drive towards goal. The defenders must then transition immediately to create a 2v2 and prevent them from scoring.

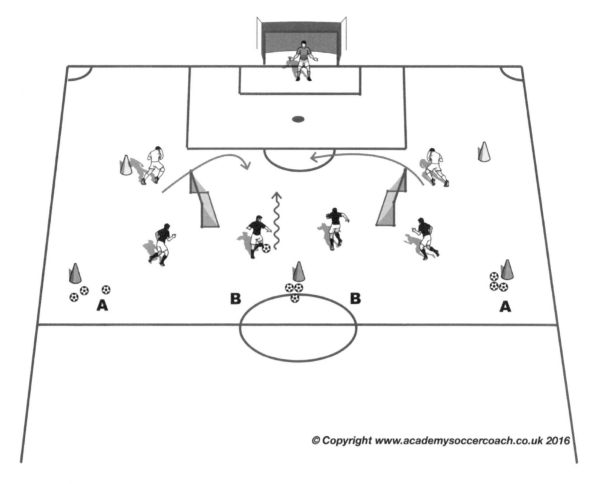

Progression:

- ✓ Allow the two wide attackers (A players) to get involved in the second attack also. Set a time limit on the attackers to score. This will create a 4v2 and will challenge the defensive players to deal with the overloads.
- ✓ Add a second mini-goal adjacent to the first one so the attacker (player A) can now attempt to beat the defender inside or outside.

Coaching Points:

- ✓ The attacker does not have to beat the defender to score; he/she can pass the ball into the mini-goal. Therefore, on the initial phase, the defenders must get their starting position quickly to cut off the middle of the field and 'show' the attacker into a 1v1 situation.
- ✓ Because there is a 6-second rule, delay becomes the goal rather than simply winning the ball. Encourage the attacker to be aggressive but patient.
- ✓ The transition from 1v1 to 1v1 must be done at maximum intensity. The defenders should attempt to get organized initially and then apply pressure as quickly as possible. Do not let the attackers have a free run into the penalty box.
- ✓ Once a 2v2 situation is created, the principles of pressure-cover-balance are applicable. Challenge the defenders to work together and communicate in this situation.

Exercise Seven

Positional Focus: Midfield 3 in a medium or low block.

Set-Up:

The exercise takes place in a 20x20 yard area, with six gates as goals. Seven players are used with three midfielders (black shirts) and four possession players (white shirts).

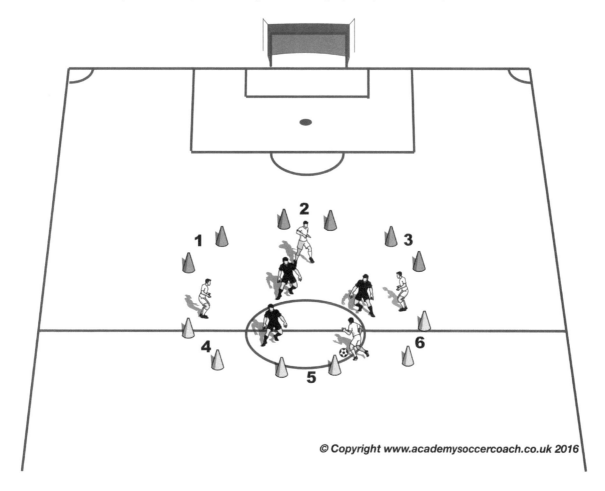

Session Details:

Both the possession (white) team and midfield (black) team are organized positionally prior to the exercise starting. The possession team take a diamond shape below and the defensive team works with one holder and two attackers. The coach can change this set-up based on their own specific game model. The exercise begins with the possession team keeping the ball and being awarded a point for 8 consecutive passes. The objective of the defensive team is to win the ball back as soon as possible and then pass the ball through one of the gates (numbered 1-6) for a point. Play for 3 minutes and then rotate defensive midfielders.

Progression:

- ✓ Once the possession team get 8 passes, award them another point if they can get a player to dribble through the gates while in control of the ball.

- ✓ Similarly, award the defensive team a point for dribbling through the gates after winning possession.

- ✓ Make the area bigger and add another midfielder (working in the middle of the diamond) to create a 5v3. This challenges the defensive players to cut off more angles and cover more ground.

Coaching Points:

- ✓ Defensive success in the game relies on the three players working together and being organized at all times. If they lose their shape, the possession team will score points. Therefore, communication is critical with all three players expected to constantly pass on information to each other.

- ✓ Focus and concentration are also very important. It is not just about chasing the ball defensively, but rather looking at cutting off options and trapping possession players when they have the ball. Once that happens, they should work aggressively to win it back.

- ✓ After winning the ball, the defensive team must provide a passing option right away. With the overload situation, it may not be possible to score a point right away. Therefore, his/her teammates must give support immediately.

Exercise Eight

<u>**Positional Focus:**</u> Two center forwards in a 4-4-2 pressing high.

<u>**Set-Up:**</u>

The exercise takes place in a 10x40 area, just outside the 18-yard box. A back four with one holding midfielder are in white, with two forwards in black. There are two mini-goals used, as well as a supply of balls to keep the session flowing.

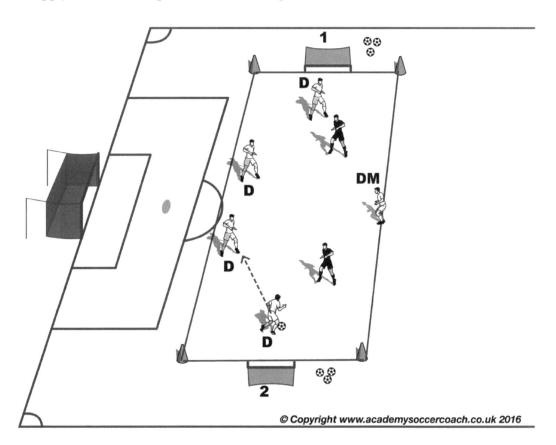

© Copyright www.academysoccercoach.co.uk 2016

<u>**Session Details:**</u>

The exercise is a 5v2 game and begins with both teams in a traditional set shape. The goal of the white team is to work the ball from one fullback to the other. Every player in the possession team is limited to two touches. The two forwards are trying to win back possession together and are awarded one point for every time they win the ball, and two points if they score into either of the mini-goals. Play for three minute sets with a two-minute recovery.

<u>**Progressions:**</u>

- ✓ Add a goalkeeper and now the forwards get three points if they transition and score in the main goal.

- ✓ Expand the area and work with three forwards now in a 4-3-3 system.

Coaching Points:

- ✓ With the possession team limited to two touches, their first touch will dictate what they are going to do with the ball. Therefore, the speed and decision making ability of both forwards must be high at all times.

- ✓ The forwards must stay connected at all times and not get split or drawn into man marking players. If they do, they will open up too much space for the switch of play.

- ✓ With a mini-goal right behind them, the rewards of pressing a fullback are very high. Therefore, this should result in forwards taking an aggressive approach to defending in those specific areas.

Exercise Nine

Set-Up:

This exercise is designed to work with wide forwards pressing against full-backs, and focuses on both cutting off passing angles and winning the ball in the challenge. Three defenders are used in black and two wide forwards are labelled A and B. The defensive goal of this specific example is to prevent passes into central areas, 'show' full-backs wide, and win the ball in a 1v1 situation.

© Copyright www.academysoccercoach.co.uk 2017

Session Details:

The coach always starts the exercise by passing the ball to the central defender. When the first pass is moving, both attackers stay at their starting positions. When the central defender passes the ball to the full-back (2), this is the trigger to initiate the press by the wide forward on the same side. Because the goal of the defending team is to stop central passes and 'show' the full-back wide, the points system is as follows: the full-back receives two points if they pass the ball into the mini-goal on that side, and 1 point if they dribble through the gate. If the wide attacker wins the ball, they receive 3 points.

The exercise can also be used as a physical challenge. As soon as the defensive action on one side is complete, the wide attacker has 5 seconds to recover back to the starting spot before the coach plays the next ball to work the other side. The center back then alternates between full-backs as players A and B take turns in resting and working. The game lasts for 3 minutes and there must be a winner.

Progressions:

- ✓ Make the distances bigger to challenge the players physically.

- ✓ Allow the center back to support the pass and limit them to one or two touches if the full-back uses them. This will challenge the wide attacker so that they must not over-commit and get beaten on a wall-pass.

- ✓ Add a goalkeeper and switch the coach for an outfield player. Now, if the wide attacker wins the ball, the server/attacker can get involved and create a 2v2 towards goal.

- ✓ Adapt the scoring to suit your system of play. Maybe you want to prevent a pass wide or a penetrating run in the middle so in that case, the mini-goal and the gates would switch places.

Coaching Points:

- ✓ The timing of the run is the first step defensively. If they make the run to press on the first pass, the center back would not play the full-back in a game situation. Instead, invite the pass wide and then aggressively press when the second pass is on the way.

- ✓ The wide forward must approach the press on an angle in order to cut off the pass first. If they press without showing an angle, the full-back has the option to beat them on either side.

- ✓ Forward momentum is with the full-back so part of the 1v1 defensive skills must be to slow down on approach, otherwise the full-back will accelerate through the gates.

Summary

✓ Pressing system is only as strong as its weakest link. Speed is a crucial component but must be supported by attitude, defensive technique, and ability to make correct decisions during the game.

✓ We cannot afford to generalize in terms of 'game intelligence' and instead have a responsibility to coach players how to thrive in this defensive system

✓ Basic and traditional exercises may not necessarily transfer automatically to the pitch. Players need position-specific work and constant feedback in order to improve and develop.

✓ Coaching points must also be extended to meet the demands of the modern game, both for positions and as a collective unit. 'Pressure - Cover - Balance' is then extended to 'Pressure - Delay - Depth - Balance'

✓ Every position has different Technical, Tactical, Mental, and Physical roles and responsibilities that must be identified in the recruiting process and communicated to every player.

✓ Work with players in the same areas of the field that they will encounter the specific challenges that you have targeted in the exercise. It will help create habits and allow the player to connect to the game itself.

✓ Position-specific training must be embedded into the training program rather than presented to the players at random moments throughout the season. If you do not see value in this training as a coach, don't expect the players to embrace it.

4
Pressing Warm-Ups

I'm a big believer that you can tell how strong a team's defensive philosophy is simply by observing the first twenty minutes of a training session. The warm-up gives so much away: the attitude of players upon arrival, intensity levels, focus, concentration, and the attention to detail from everyone involved. If success leaves clues, there are quite a few of them dropped right here. The role of the coach is critical in this process and he/she must be intentional about everything that takes place in the session. Rondo's are a perfect example of this. Many teams have watched Barcelona zip the ball around and thought "if they do it, we should be doing the same." They implement those exercises into their daily training session but fail to govern it with any intent or purpose. As a result, players stroll up to the grid, stand around, joke as they make simple technical mistakes, and play without any purpose or tactical thought. However, the Barcelona and Guardiola's teams, approach them very differently. Player's body shape in possession and the angles of defensive pairings are constantly under scrutiny, and coaches restart the games so quickly that technique and decision making are tested at a high level. They may be similar exercises but they are vastly different in the approach from the coaching staff, and this leads to very different results. This is an example of intentional growth versus accidental growth.

The foundation of pressing is centered around working at your maximum and aggressively pushing your limits, both individually and collectively. Therefore, everything we do on the training pitch either strengthens our system or contradicts it. Without doubt, a sluggish warm-up goes against that philosophy in every way possible. Instead of letting our players choose their attitude for the day, we must condition them, through the environment we create, to compete at their best from the first minute of the session in the same way the game will demand. Although slow training exercises may result in fewer mistakes and can sometimes be more aesthetically pleasing, you don't want mistakes to eventually come out under the pressure of competition.

If you want to get the most out of a pressing session possible, you cannot compromise on the following:

- Effort
- Intensity
- Focus
- Competitiveness

Intensity Drivers

Intensity and pressing go hand in hand. You cannot expect a team to hunt the ball effectively if they lack important traits like energy and a passion for hard work. Even the best teams can struggle to bring high intensity levels every day of the week, so the coach must sometimes play a part and inject it into the training session. Regardless of ability and level, I believe that the 3 C's drive intensity:

1. Clock – Every game and/or exercise is timed, usually in increments of five minutes or below. I am a big believer that time should be used to challenge and stimulate players' thinking, instead of as a guideline to how close they are to being finished. If exercises or sessions go on for too long, tempo and quality will typically drop.

2. Competition – If you want to have a competitive team, they must practice winning every single day. When there is an urgency from everyone to win, players will hold each other accountable and you have a chance of replicating the pressure of performance that they will experience in a game.

3. Communication – If there is volume and energy in the training session, the chances are the tempo will be quite high. Then you can channel that enthusiasm into positively impacting performance. For example, what type of information are we sending to each other?

Pressing Warm-Up Coaching Principles:

If a warm-up can make or break a pressing session, we must get the small details right as coaches. Therefore, coaching principles are now extended beyond tactical or technical concepts. The following must be considered if a coach wants to hit the ground running and maximize their pressing sessions.

- **Create a Common Language** - Be consistent in the words you use to describe defensive actions so that players can associate and connect them to the game and tactical concepts. Be intentional about the language used in the early parts of the session.
- **Quick Ball Movement** - Even if the session is not focussed on possession, you need the ball to move quickly in order to challenge the players defensively. Again, think of Pep Guardiola's rondos and how adamant he is that the ball moves with pace and quality.
- **Maximum Defensive Actions** - These are short, intense games that are designed to constantly shape and reinforce defensive behaviours. All defending should be aggressive and distances should be very close so that we can challenge defenders to be aggressive in both technique and mentality throughout the session.
- **Use of Recovery Time** - Use the recovery time to make your coaching points rather than stopping the session constantly and then have players stand around during intervals. Allow them to physically recover during the warm-up, but challenge their ability to receive information so that they do not have an opportunity to 'switch off' in the beginning.
- **Organization** - Always make sure there is a supply of balls so that the exercises can restart in a matter of seconds. This will constantly challenge players to transition, recover, refocus, and set high standards early in the session.
- **Energy** - Always remember that it's not natural for players to get excited about a defending session. The players will need some help here, so if the coaching staff want a high energy pressing session, they must make sure they bring passion, enthusiasm, and intensity to the pitch. Players will feed off the energy that the coaches show and this will be even more important when fatigue kicks in.

Exercise One

Set-Up:

This exercise allows you to define the difference between aggressive and passive defending. It also allows players to appreciate distances and angles in 1v1 defending. The set-up is very simple. Players are organized into pairs inside a 20x20 yard area. The player with the ball is the attacker and the player without the ball is the defender.

Session Details:

Players on opposite teams pair up and stay together throughout the exercise. It has a low-tempo start with the defensive player jockeying the attacker for 15-20 seconds as he/she dribbles around the square. On the coach's random signal, the intensity switches dramatically as the defender has ten seconds to win the ball and knock it outside of the square. If the defender wins it, he/she gets a point. If they fail to win it, the attacker gets the point. The exercise restarts again. Play for four minutes and then switch roles. Play three sets and keep score throughout.

Progressions:

- ✓ If the defender fouls the attacking player, the attacker gets two points. This is to instil discipline in the defending and make defenders aware that there are greater consequences to fouling than simply getting beat.

- ✓ As a coach, you can manipulate the intensity of the exercise by adjusting the times or the distances. For example, expanding the square to 40x40 yards would be a much greater challenge physically for both players.

- ✓ Have the attacker turn around on the coach's signal and the defensive player now has to win possession as the attacker shields the ball. This is another situation that can appear in a game within a pressing situation.

- ✓ Offer defenders an incentive to win their ball and help win another by 'doubling up' on a different attacker.

Coaching Points:

- ✓ Players must understand why the attacker gets the point even if they don't get beaten in a 1v1 situation. This is about winning the ball and forcing a mistake from the attacking player.

- ✓ Body position is critical for a defender here. They are going to have to learn how to get tight and physical without fouling (use of their arms) and the value of showing the attacker into a corner or wide area.

- ✓ The ten second rule is designed to add urgency to the defending, but not desperation. The defender should not be diving in to win the ball immediately and should create an opportunity with their feet and body where they can win the ball without the element of high risk.

Exercise Two

<u>Set-Up:</u>

This is a quick transition game that can be used as a warm-up activity or an early season exercise to explain key movements and establishing what kind of intensity you want from your team in pressing. Play takes place inside two 20x20 areas, with a 5-yard corridor in the middle. Eighteen players are organized into three teams of six.

<u>Session Details:</u>

Two attacking teams start in grids at either side and the defensive team starts in the middle channel. The coach starts the exercise by triggering the ball into one of the two grids. Once the ball arrives inside, the defensive team sends three players to go and press the ball aggressively. If the defending team wins the ball, the team who loses possession now becomes the defensive team and another ball is triggered immediately into the other grid. After the team in possession of the ball complete ten passes they can transfer the ball to the other grid, either over the top or through the middle channel (the three players in the middle can intercept it). If the possession team is successful with the switch of play, the other three players in the middle must now sprint and defend. Play three sets of four minute games.

Progressions:

- ✓ Introduce a scoring system: Award a point to the team who switches the play successfully after ten passes.

- ✓ To increase the technical demands of the exercise, the teams in possession have a two-touch limit – or one-touch for a short pass and two touches for a switch of play.

- ✓ You can change the structure of the game where now one team is the all-time defending team and must win 5 balls back in total. For every ten passes the teams in possession get, the coach adds an additional ball to the defending team.

Coaching Points:

- ✓ It is a game of constant attacking and defensive transitions so defensive reactions must always be positive and fast. Delays due to disappointment or loss of focus can hurt teams so challenge players to minimize those.

- ✓ There should be constant communication throughout the exercise, especially for the defensive team. This should be fast paced, competitive, and enjoyable so everyone must contribute.

- ✓ Challenge the defensive team to have an organization with their pressing, and see if they can both force and keep the possession team into corners in order to limit their space and passing options.

- ✓ The long ball (switch) should always be pressured, even if a defensive player cannot get close enough to block. Minimal pressure can be the difference between a comfortable pass and a mistake so do not allow teams to give up after ten passes. It is the switch that costs points!

Exercise Three

Set-Up:

This transition game challenges players both technically and physically. It takes place in a 20x20 yard area, with the field split in half. Twelve players are split into two teams. The coach needs a supply of balls to keep the tempo high and challenge the players.

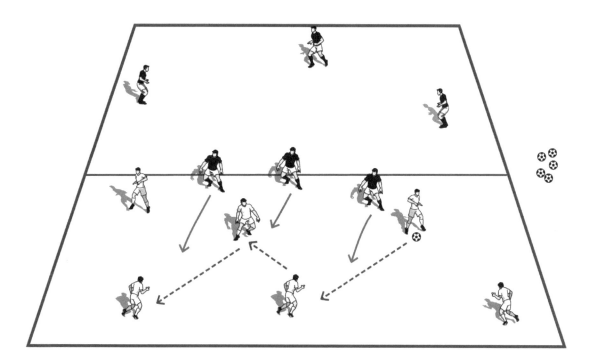

© Copyright www.academysoccercoach.co.uk 2016

Session Details:

Each team is assigned one half of the field. The coach starts the exercise by triggering a ball to either team. As soon as the ball is played, three players from the other half can go into the area and defend. The team in possession must get ten passes for a point. The three defending players must simply win the ball. If they do, the coach immediately restarts the game in the other half and the other team must now defend. The first team to ten points wins. Play three games in total.

Progressions:

✓ You cannot use the same three defensive players over and over again. Challenge teams to organize and constantly communicate throughout the game. If you want to really make it difficult – implement a condition where they must have different combinations of three defensive players so that they cannot simply rotate.

✓ To increase the technical demands of the exercise, the teams in possession have a one or two touch limit.

✓ You can change the physical or technical demands by increasing or decreasing the playing area size and/or defensive numbers.

Coaching Points:

✓ In a small area and with points awarded for pass completion, the pressure must be ultra-aggressive. Do not allow defensive players to 'stand-off' or delay players in possession. Once they can apply pressure, they should be competing for the ball.

✓ The speed of transitions plays a critical role to a team's success in this game. If they are slow (either mentally or physically) to react to possession being lost, the opposition can already have passes completed and win easy points.

Exercise Four

Set-Up:

This exercise is perfect for a warm-up exercise or to teach the functions of forwards or midfields who are pressing in a wide or central area. It is a directional possession game which punishes teams who do not get their defensive organization right. The game is played in a 40x40 yard square with small coned areas in each corner. Twelve players are used and are organized into two teams of six.

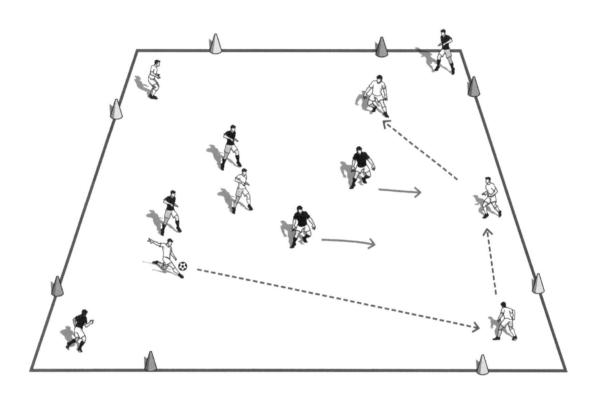

Session Details:

Both teams are organized into four players in the middle and two players on the outside, diagonally facing each other. It is a directional possession game with the objective of both teams to work the ball from one corner to the other. Players in the corners must stay there and are limited to two or one touch, depending on the level. Do not allow the players on the outside to stop the ball dead before making the passing decision as this will kill the tempo of the game. The players in the middle have unlimited touches. A team is awarded a point by transferring the ball from one corner to the other. The defensive team must press to stop the switch and then look to transition immediately and do the same thing. There should be four games lasting four minutes each, with a one-minute recovery after each one.

Progressions:

✓ Making the playing area bigger increases the physical demands of the defending team. It also challenges them to prevent longer diagonal passes that will beat the press.

✓ After the player on the outside passes the ball back into the middle, they join the 4v4 game there and the player who passed them the ball initially must take their place.

Coaching Points:

✓ Because the game has a directional component to it, the pressing must be organized and defensive players must prevent teams from playing out of corners.

✓ There is a high reward to winning the ball closer to your team's corner, therefore the pressing should be aggressive and attack-minded.

✓ Once teams win possession, can they keep it and connect a pass to allow their team to transition offensively? If they are effective at this, they have a great opportunity to dictate the tempo of the game.

Exercise Five

Set-Up:

This warm-up exercise will teach players the value of distances and angles when they are pressing. Eight players are split into four teams of two. The play takes place in a 10x10 yard square, which can be adapted to the level of the players. It is always a good idea to have a good supply of balls so the game can flow quickly and the players are tested physically.

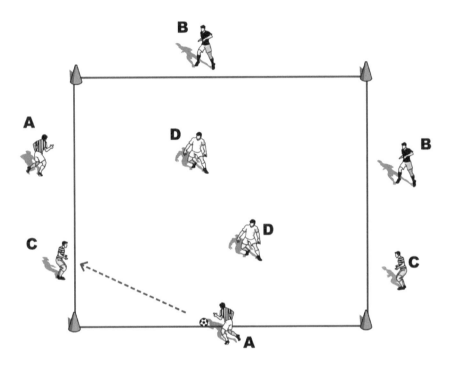

Session Details:

Players work in pairs throughout this exercise. The game starts with one pair in the middle who will act as defenders. The exercise is simple to organize and begins in a traditional 6v2 rondo, with the outside players limited to two touches. If the defensive pair win the ball, they switch roles with the player who gave the ball away and their partner. If the defensive pair are split at any time of the rondo, they stay in for an extra set. For every ten completed passes from the outside players, the defensive pair are awarded a point. Play 4x 4 minute games and the team with the least amount of points is the winner.

Progressions:

- ✓ To put more of a tactical emphasis on the rondo, you can adjust the shape to a 20x10 yard area and organize the players positionally, i.e. central players on single lines and wide players doubling up.

- ✓ Add an extra player into the middle who acts as a pivot player, trying to play in between the defenders.

- ✓ To increase the technical demands of the exercise, the teams in possession have a one or two touch limit.

Coaching Points:

- ✓ There are two goals for defensive players:
  - o Do not allow the ball to go round the square in a clock-like motion and find a new player with every pass.
  - o Do not get caught flat and allow a pass to split both defensive players.

- ✓ There must be communication throughout the defensive phase and constant reminders about who is stepping and who is providing cover.

- ✓ Make sure the transitions are at full speed at all times. Do not allow players to jog or walk into defensive transition. Restart the games fast and challenge them to focus quickly.

- ✓ In a 6v2 scenario, especially after 2 or 3 minute's work, it may be difficult to press every pass. However, when the outside players get to 7 passes, they must be working at their maximum in order to prevent unwanted points being awarded.

Exercise Six

Set-Up:

This exercise was designed by Lee Woodward and focuses on playing against an overload and preventing the ball being transferred from one side of the pitch to the other. A 20x10 yard area is used and split into four 10x5 yard grids. Twelve players are split into three teams with one player in each grid.

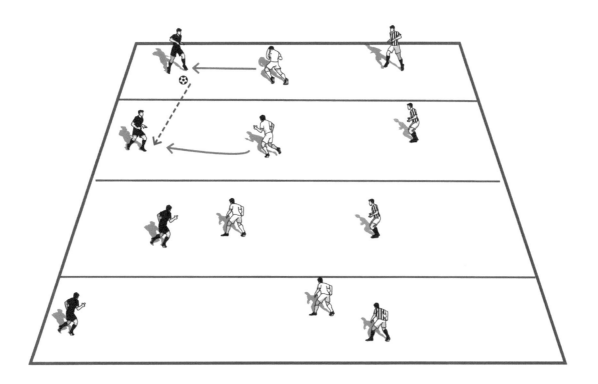

© Copyright www.academysoccercoach.co.uk 2017

Session Details:

At the start of the exercise, one team is designated as the defending team, which creates a 2v1 in each grid. The goal of the two teams in possession is to work the ball from one side to the other (left to right above). All defensive players are limited to one grid each and must maintain a team shape that prevents a player from opening up and avoids getting split with one pass. The attacking players can play back into the same grid to keep possession. If the defensive players win the ball, the team that lost possession become defenders and the game transitions quickly.

Progressions:

✓ Limit the team in possession to two touches.

✓ Make the playing area bigger to increase the physical demands of the pressing team.

✓ Allow two defending players in the same grid at one time so that they must now work together as a team to shift over and cover space quickly.

✓ Add a mini goal on both ends and now the possession team are trying to work the ball into the goal.

Coaching Points:

✓ The objective of the defender inside the grid with the ball is to block the ball from advancing to a new grid. Therefore, defensive body shape must be correct and positioning should never be flat.

✓ Supporting defensive players must be aware of distances throughout the game. Because they are dealing with an overload, they must not get dragged towards the side of the ball, otherwise they will get split.

✓ Challenge the defensive team to work together and communicate constantly throughout the exercise.

Exercise Seven

Set-Up:

This exercise takes place inside a 30x30 yard area and is a 3v2 game with two objectives for the defensive players:

- Defending against an overload
- Pressing without getting exposed in the space behind

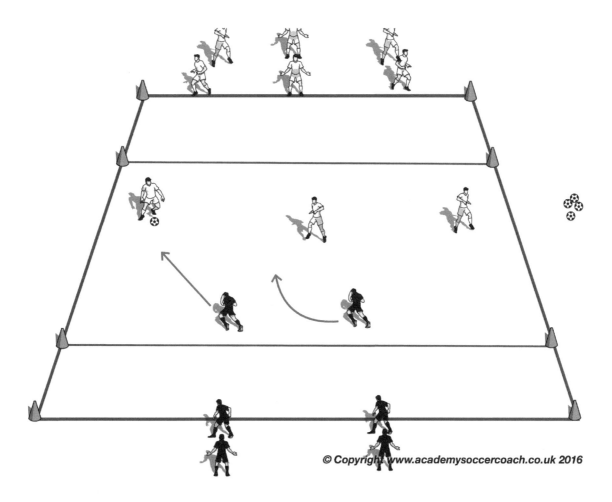

© Copyright www.academysoccercoach.co.uk 2016

Session Details:

Players are organized into two teams. The attackers are in black shirts and the defenders are in white shirts. Coach begins the exercise by passing a ball to the first attacking group of three players. When the initial ball is moving, this is the trigger for the defensive pair to press high and apply initial pressure at maximum speed. In the 3v2 scenario, the goal of the attacking team is to dribble the ball into the end zone. They can also pass the ball into the end zone, but the attacking player cannot be standing inside it before the ball is played. They are awarded one point for this. The goal of the defensive pair is to win the ball and counter by dribbling into the attackers' end zone in transition. They are awarded two points every time they achieve this. Play for 3 x 3 minute games and keep the score throughout.

Progressions:

- ✓ Increase the spaces and add both a defender and attacker, creating a 4v3.

- ✓ Implement a time limit on the attacking team, which should increase attacking penetration and challenge the defenders vertically, rather than horizontally.

Coaching Points:

- ✓ Initial position is crucial for the defensive pair. If they are slow in getting out to the ball, the attackers can advance the ball and exploit spaces in behind. Therefore, distances are so important in the pressure phase and the attackers should not have time or space to look forward and find a penetrating pass.

- ✓ Body shape is also important for the defensive pair when they press. They must try to turn the 3v2 game into a 2v2 game so should 'show' attackers into a wide area and then try to keep them there. If the central attacker has the ball, it is going to be very difficult for the defenders.

- ✓ The distance of the second defender is an important coaching point. Too close to the first defender and they will get exposed on the weak side. Too far away and they leave space for the inside run and cannot provide cover. They must understand the importance of this and get the balance right.

Summary

- ✓ We are what we repeatedly do. A team that embraces hard work on a consistent basis, has a great chance of producing the right kind of performance at the weekend.

- ✓ A coach cannot expect players to display intensity, desire, and quality during a training session if they do not demand it from the first minute.

- ✓ It is very difficult to chase intensity and tempo twenty minutes into the session. Typically, if it's not there by that stage, teams struggle for the remainder and the session is wasted or falls short in quality.

- ✓ The 3 C's (Clock, Competition, and Communication) are decisive in driving intensity during the training sessions.

- ✓ If the ball does not move quickly and with quality during the warm-up, the players are not going to get tested defensively. Therefore, intensity is required both in and out of possession if the players are going to be challenged.

- ✓ Challenge players to remain focused throughout and use the recovery time to apply coaching points or remind players of roles and responsibilities. Be careful of conditioning players to lose concentration when they are not pressing.

5
Gegenpressing

"I believe that Barcelona's outstanding performance is based on the way the whole team, with abandon and passion, tried to win the ball back after a turnover." Thomas Tuchel

It has become one of the most talked-about themes in the coaching world over the past five years. Gegenpressing, also known as counter-pressing, means to pressure the opposition as a collective group immediately after losing the ball. So instead of dropping off to reorganize and focus on the defensive shape, high intensity pressure is immediately applied around the ball in both an aggressive and organized manner. The entire team must play a role in winning the ball back and not just one or two players. Again, it is not a new concept but has been redefined in recent years and used to devastating effect by Thomas Tuchel, Marcelo Bielsa, Jurgen Klopp, Mauricio Pochettino, and Pep Guardiola.

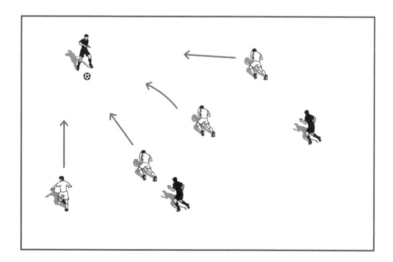

"The best moment to win the ball is immediately after your team just lost it. The opponent is still looking for orientation where to pass the ball. He will have taken his eyes off the game to make his tackle or interception and he will have expended energy. Both make him vulnerable." – Jurgen Klopp

There are two goals of gegenpressing:

1. Win the ball back as quickly as possible and counter attack.
2. Force the opposition into a rushed or inaccurate pass, which then allows you to gain possession in another area of the field.

"Think about the passes you have to make to get a player in a No 10 role in a position where he can play the genius pass. Counter-pressing lets you win back the ball nearer to the goal. It's only one pass away from a really good opportunity. No playmaker in the world can be as good as a good counter pressing situation. That shows why it's so important." Jurgen Klopp

Why Do It?

"In the first moment of defending, there are no formations." Jurgen Klopp

- It prevents opponents counter attacking opportunities.
- Your opponent is most vulnerable when their defensive organization is not established. By winning the ball back, the opposition's shape is in transition and that usually means plenty of spaces available to exploit.
- The opposition have just expended energy in their defensive efforts to win the ball, and therefore may be looking to recover physically with the ball in possession. They may not want, or have the capacity for, another intense action.
- You can provide more defensive stability higher up the field if you can press immediately. If teams attempt to drop and retreat, they become reactive to the opposition and invite more players on the opposition to join the attack.
- You gain possession of the ball higher up the field, with the possibility of creating a goal-scoring opportunity immediately.
- Today's players are fitter than they have ever been and have the physical ability to press harder and longer than they have ever done before.

Negatives

- It is very much a high-risk strategy. If your players are not physically or mentally equipped to react at the right times, the opposition can play out and exploit numerical advantages in key areas of the field.
- If one player does not commit to the work, the entire structure collapses. It needs eleven players to work, including a goalkeeper who can make correct decisions and is comfortable playing high up the field.
- There are no set triggers or pressing points, so the workload can be constant and exhausting.

"The longer we have the ball, the less can happen against you. Then you lose it and you need to get it back, I thought it's a good idea to get it back immediately, because it makes life easier. That is why we think counter-pressing is really important, but it doesn't work all the time, so then you have to defend in a different way. That's how football works – you close one hole, unfortunately you open another one. It never ends, it never ends!" - Jurgen Klopp

How Do You Coach It?

It may have a simple definition, but without a doubt, gegenpressing is a very complex system to coach and apply effectively on the pitch. As we discussed in previous chapters, your play model becomes crucial in pressing because that will be the starting position for so many defensive opportunities to regain the ball. When it comes to gegenpressing, that becomes even more important, along with additional tactical, technical, mental, and physical components. Below are ten principles to successful gegenpressing:

1. There must be an understanding of playing style and system before the moment of possession.
2. Your team must be compact – vertically and laterally.
3. If you do not have enough numbers in the same area as the ball, gegenpressing simply will not work.
4. You need at least 3-5 players around the ball immediately after possession is lost.
5. Players who cannot press the ball immediately, must drop into a recovery position instantly.
6. At Barcelona, Pep Guardiola used a "one and three" principle when the ball is lost. One player goes to the ball and applies pressure, and three go into the same area to try and cut out passing angles.
7. There must be positive and aggressive reaction to the ball being lost. The team must move forward as a unit immediately.
8. Player closest to the ball must apply immediate and aggressive pressure, without diving in, allowing penetration, or conceding a 'soft' free kick.
9. As a team, you must always cut off the middle of the pitch.
10. Once possession is won back there are two decisions to make:
    - Are you in a position to counter attack?
    - If not, can you keep possession?

"In the middle of the field, the opponent has more options when it comes to rotation, field of vision, and passing. Even if a player arcs their run to block one side of the field, the opponent will have the other entire half of the field to work with. Ideally, the opponent who recovers the ball will be forced in the direction of the touchline or back towards his own goal and away from the center of the field. There, he will have no opportunity to rotate and his choices will be limited, which will also rob him of the most effective and quickest path towards goal, as any counterattack will take longer." – Rene Maric

Coverage Variant

Analyst Rene Maric writes for spielverlagerung.com which posts detailed tactical analysis for coaches (the site is a must for all coaches who are looking to develop and improve their knowledge of the game). Rene has done extensive work in this area and has developed four counter-pressing variants for various coverages.

- ## *Man-Oriented Gegenpressing*

In this style of pressing, every player looks for a player to cover as soon as their team concedes possession. The player runs towards and cuts off their opponent, and forces them into a follow-up action. The goal of this style of gegenpressing is to put the opposition under immediate pressure and trap them in a situation where they cannot escape the pressure. This style was used by Jupp Heynckes when he was at Bayern Munich.

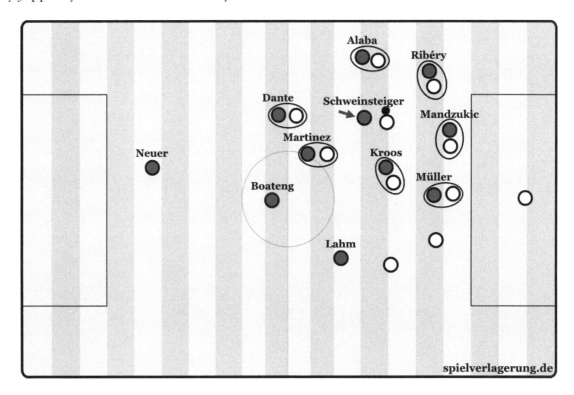

- ## *Leeway-Oriented Counterpressing*

In this style of pressing, there is little or no focus on the opposition players. Instead, full attention goes to the player in possession of the ball and that area of the field. The entire defensive team attempts to put as much pressure inside a certain area, which should force mistakes and take away short passing options for the player in possession. The goal is for the player in possession to turn the ball over immediately, or send it long. This style has been used by Jurgen Klopp at Dortmund and Liverpool.

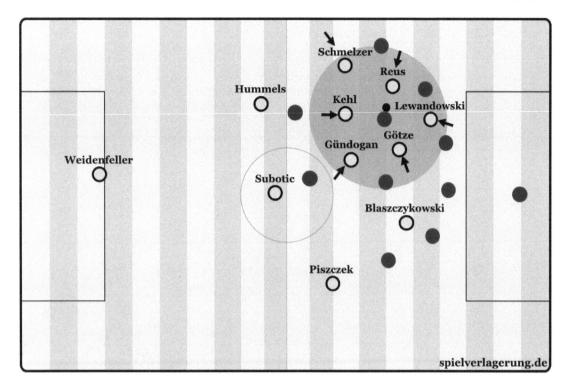

- ## *Passing Lane-Oriented Gegenpressing*

Although the possession team is placed under intense pressure with this style, the key difference here is that the opposition are allowed to attempt the first pass. Although the passer is not aggressively attacked, the pass certainly is. The goal here is to block passing lanes and allow two players to potentially press the player who receives the ball. Barcelona used this style of pressing under Pep Guardiola.

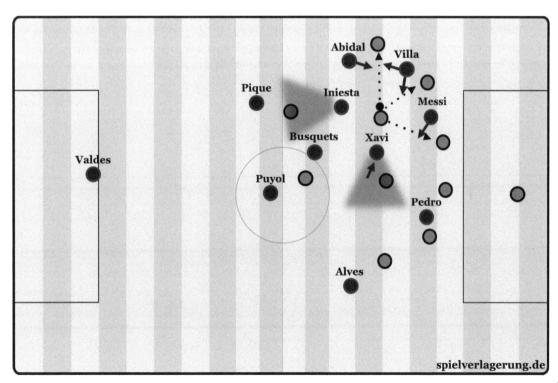

- ***Ball-Oriented Gegenpressing***

With this style, a team simply goes towards the ball, with no regard for shape or positioning. Although the levels of aggression and speed can be quite high here, it is a vulnerable style. It was used by Ajax and the Netherlands in the 1970s, and also by SV Grodig under Adi Hutter.

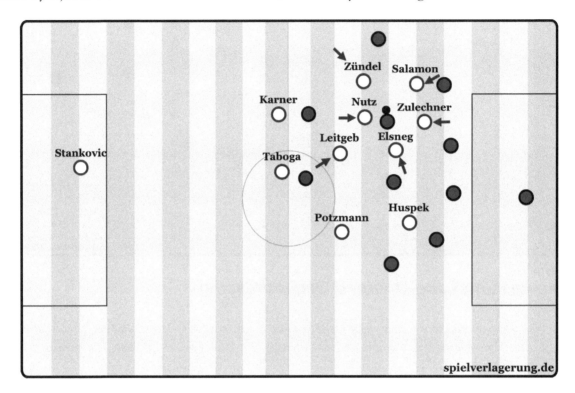

"One must not assume – and as a coach must not require – that a certain style of cover always be used. It usually depends on the situation and the options available, which are presented by a team's shape and the type of lost ball. In most cases, it is a mixture of these four coverages." – Rene Maric

Exercise One

Set-Up:

This exercise takes place in a 20x20 yard area with 4 gates (A, B,C,D) inside the playing area, each 2 yards apart. Twelve players are involved and split into three teams of four players each. Each team has one ball. Coach will need a supply of balls also for the progression.

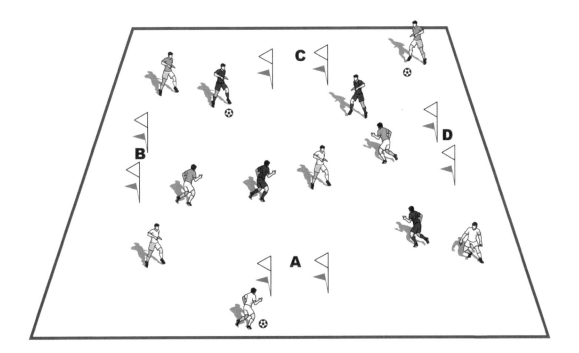

Session Details:

The exercise begins with each team passing the ball between themselves. As a coach, you will want a high level of tempo for the exercise so challenge players to move the ball quickly, good weight on the pass, and then take new positions. The coach will provide the trigger for transition by calling out a color of one of the teams. The team whose color is called now have sole possession of the ball, the other two balls are dead. The team in possession of the ball is trying to dribble through one of the four gates immediately, while the other two teams must react quickly and prevent them from scoring. In other words, upon transition the game turns into a 4v8. After the ball is won back or a goal is scored, play restarts again with one ball each.

"GREEN!"

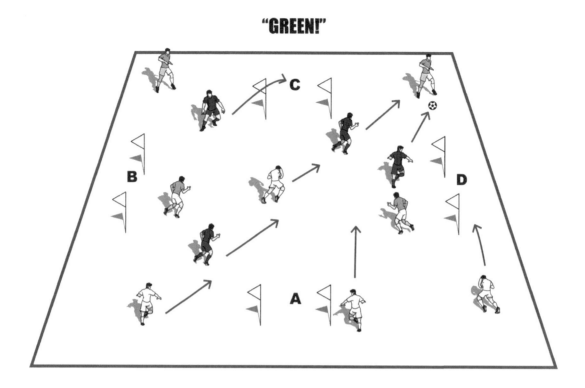

Progression:

✓ Once the first ball is won back, the coach will then serve another ball to another player in the same team. This progression simulates a team breaking the initial press and then having to transition offensively.

✓ Expand the size of the area to increase the physical challenges.

Coaching Points:

✓ Because of the possession component of the exercise, many players will focus entirely on the ball. Instead, you want them to be aware of where the other two balls are so that they will react quicker upon the coach's signal.

✓ Communication can help teams establish who is responsible for pressing initially, especially with the progression.

Exercise Two

Set-Up:

This exercise takes place in a 20x20 yard area, with four mini-goals on the outside. Twelve players are divided into three teams of four. Coach will need a supply of balls to keep the exercise flowing at all times.

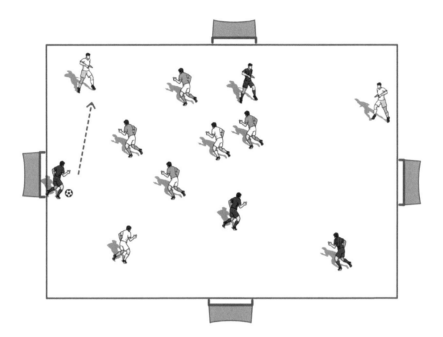

© Copyright www.academysoccercoach.co.uk 2016

Session Details:

It begins as an 8v4 exercise with two teams keeping possession against one pressing team. The goal of the pressing team is to win the ball back immediately and score in any one of the four goals. Each team will defend for three minutes, but in order to keep the intensity levels high, play three sets of one minute, with a thirty second recovery period in between each one. After each team has worked for three minutes, switch the pressing team with one of the possession teams.

The scoring system works as follows:

1. If the eight players in possession get eight passes, the defensive team loses one point.
2. If the pressing team win the ball and score in one of the goals, they get two points.
3. The team with the most points win.

<u>Progression:</u>

- ✓ Add a small 3x3 yard square into the middle of the playing area. Now if the team in possession can pass the ball into the square and transfer it out in another direction, the defending team loses two points. The objective here is to challenge the pressing team not to get split and constantly keep defensive shape in relation to the position of the ball.

<u>Coaching Points:</u>

- ✓ In any gegenpressing activity, urgency to win the ball must be a priority. This urgency must be evident in all four players, not just two or three. Therefore, as a coach, you must identify which players are simply occupying a central area of the field and not looking to help their team win the ball back. Once you identify those players, constantly encourage them to commit to the required work.

- ✓ Shape is critical for the defensive team also. Even if they are all working at their maximum, they will not be successful unless they can keep their shape.

- ✓ You do not want:
    - ○ Possession continuously going around in a circle (this would simulate a team constantly switching the play in a game).
    - ○ Players passing back to where the ball came from (this would simulate pressing flat and easily allowing players to beat the press).

- ✓ In terms of shape, encourage the four defensive players to send the ball into corners and then press aggressively to cut off all angles. The corners should limit the choices of the player in possession, as well as the reward of a goal if you successfully win the ball.

- ✓ Communication is important for the pressing team to establish immediate pressure and shape. They must give information and energy to one another, and not simply rely on the coach to constantly instruct throughout.

Exercise Three

Set-Up:

This exercise takes place in a 20x20 yard grid which is divided into four areas, with a smaller 5x5 yard square in the middle. Players are organized into two teams of eight players. Coach will need a supply of balls for quick restarts and to keep intensity levels as high as possible.

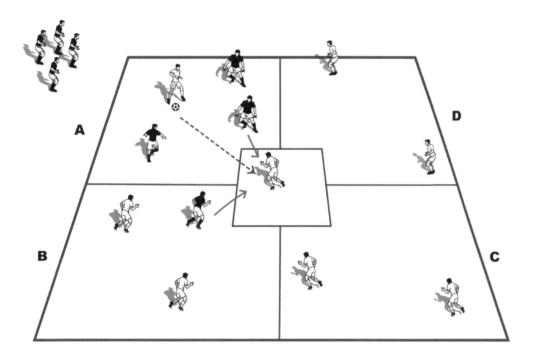

Session Details:

One team begins as the possession team (white team above) in an 8v4 game. Four players in the defensive team (black team) work at one time, while the other four players recover. The goal of the defensive team is to press and prevent the following:

- The ball being circulated around four squares either clockwise or counter-clockwise. This is to challenge the defensive team to stop the switch of play through the opposition midfield or defensive lines.
- The team in possession passes the ball into a player in the middle square, who then transfers it into another square. This is to replicate the holding midfielder opening up and switching the play.

If either of these conditions occur, the team in possession are awarded one point. If the defensive team successfully win the ball, another one is triggered immediately from the coach. After 90 seconds, the defensive team rotates four players on and off and the game continues quickly. Then teams switch roles and the defensive team become the possession team and vice-versa.

Progression:

- ✓ To increase the physical demands of the game, you can adapt the playing time to 2 minutes and/or increase the size of the field.
- ✓ In order to further incentivize the defensive team to win the ball, position each one of the four recovering players on the defensive team in each corner of the main area (see below). Now if the pressing team win the ball back and can pass to one of the players in a corner, the possession team lose a point.

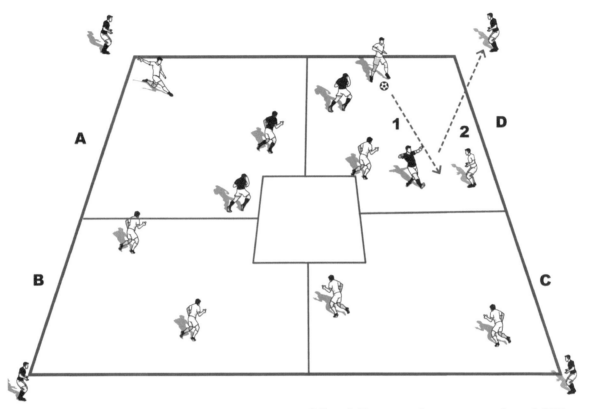

© Copyright www.academysoccercoach.co.uk 2016

Coaching Points:

- ✓ The scoring system demands that the pressing team must pay special attention to two tactical factors in the game:
    1. Players must 'show' and press the ball in the direction where it came from. Do not let the player on the ball find a 'new' pass but rather show them back to where they came from.
    2. When the ball is played into the middle square, there should be immediate pressure from the defensive team.
- ✓ Because of the demands above, there needs to be constant work rate and problem solving from the defensive team. Do not let any player become detached from their team defensively or 'check out' mentally.
- ✓ Encourage the players on the outside to communicate information to the defensive team. They can help pass on information and keep intensity levels high, as well as seeing situations that they will also be experiencing.

Exercise Four

Set-Up:

The exercise takes place in a 30x30 yard grid which is divided into four 10x10yard areas, A, B, C, and D. Players are organized into two teams of eight players. Coach will need a supply of balls for quick restarts and to keep intensity levels as high as possible.

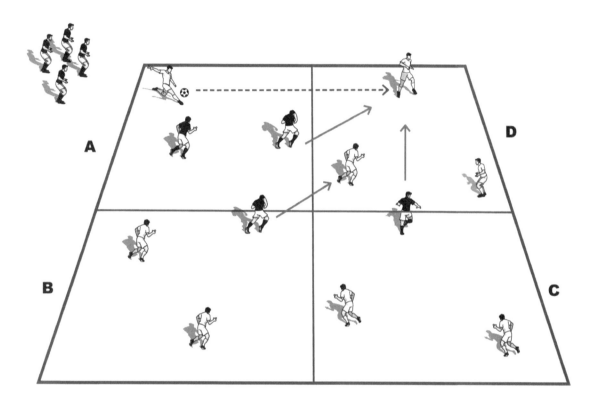

© Copyright www.academysoccercoach.co.uk 2016

Session Details:

One team begins as the possession team (white team above) in an 8v4 game. Four players in the defensive team (black team) work at one time, while the other four players recover. As the team in possession keeps the ball, the defending team must have all four players inside the same square that the ball is in within 6 seconds of the first pass. If the defending team fail to do so, the possession team scores a point. If the defending team wins the ball, play restarts from the coach with another ball immediately. After two minutes, the four defensive players rotate with their teammates and after both sets defend, the teams switch roles. Play four sets and keep the score throughout.

<u>Progressions:</u>

- ✓ To increase the physical demands of the game, you can adapt the playing time to 3 minutes and/or increase the size of the field.

- ✓ If the team in possession switch the play diagonally (e.g. from A to C, or B to D, or vice versa) the defending team loses another point. This is to stop the possession team from playing longer passes and/or playing through the middle.

- ✓ You can challenge the defending team to possess in transition once they win the ball. If they get three consecutive passes, they are rewarded with a point.

<u>Coaching Points:</u>

- ✓ The game demands that the team shifts together, but because the team in possession will attempt to switch the ball, the distances are going to have to be very close. Defensive players must therefore not allow attacking players to get their heads up and see/play a lofted pass.

- ✓ Although the defensive team must work together, they must also have a shape and balance. There should always be a defensive player a little bit deeper in the square to avoid splitting passes and penetration.

- ✓ When the defensive win the ball and the coach restarts the game quickly, what is the reaction of the defensive team? This is a key moment in the game as it will determine their mindset to a loss in possession immediately after a regain. If they can excel in this moment, they can transfer it to a game situation.

Exercise Five

Set-Up:

This exercise takes place in a 20x50 yard area with a 5-yard end zone on each side. Players are divided into two teams of six and there are two keepers, who will take up position inside each end zone. Coach will need a supply of balls to keep the session flowing and the intensity levels high.

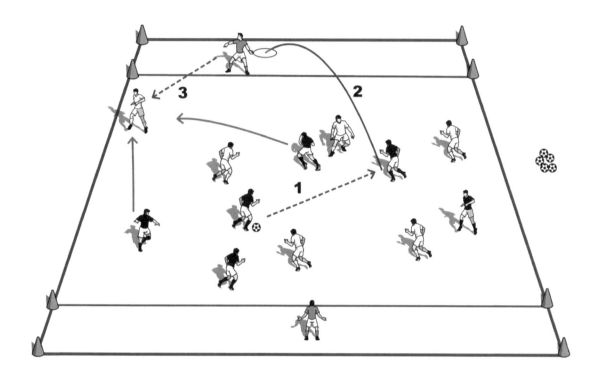

Session Details:

Teams play a 6v6 possession game inside the area. The goal for the team in possession is to work the ball towards the keeper on either end zone. They must find the keeper's hands with a chipped or lofted pass. A completed pass without bouncing earns the possession team a point.

The moment of transition arises as soon as a point is scored. The goalkeeper must then play the ball to the opposing team who now try to score at the other end, and the team who just scored now have to transition defensively and begin to press. The nature of the game demands that defensive pressure is immediate because any time and space should result in a scoring opportunity. If the team in possession fail in their attempt to score by either missing the goalkeeper or if the ball bounces, a new ball is triggered by the coach and possession turns over to the other team.

Progressions:

- ✓ You can make the game more difficult in possession by increasing the length of the field so that players in possession cannot score from deep. This will add a build-up element to the game.

- ✓ Again, to increase difficulty level defensively, enforce a pass limit on the team in possession so that the game does not become a series of transitions from attempted lofted passes to either keeper.

- ✓ Add two neutral players who occupy each wide channel and can offer an additional passing option to the team in possession. This will challenge the defensive team in how they press. Do they show outside or inside? Coach can decide whether the defensive team can win the ball from the neutral players.

Coaching Points:

- ✓ If the players have the ability to score from deep then the pressure on the ball has to be high, with special attention to distances. Too much space will result in easy scoring opportunities so it is important that players understand exactly what level of pressure the game demands.

- ✓ The moment of transition, directly after scoring, will determine the success of a team defensively in this exercise. How quickly do they react? How many players go and press the ball? How aggressively are they pressing? Challenge players to be aware of and excel in this moment.

- ✓ There will inevitably be breakdowns defensively when the scoring team must transition to pressing. High levels of communication can prevent these breakdowns, help solve them when they occur, and raise defensive intensity levels.

Exercise Six

Set-Up:

The exercise takes place in a 20x40 yard grid which is split into two areas. There are two teams of eight players. Coach will need a supply of balls for quick restarts and to keep intensity levels as high as possible.

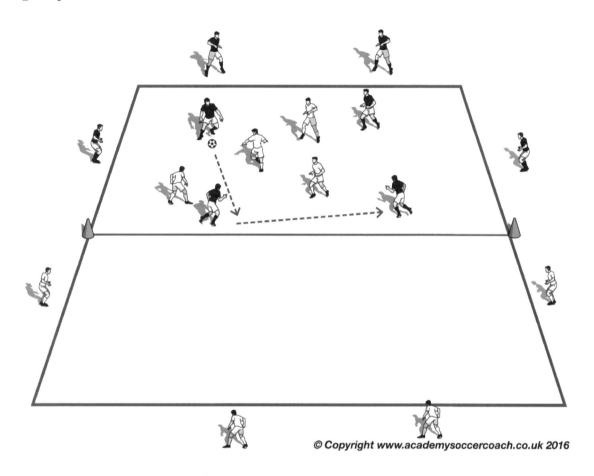

© Copyright www.academysoccercoach.co.uk 2016

Session Details:

Each team is assigned one half of the field, with four players on the inside and four players on the outside. As the coach triggers the ball into the black team above, the four white players must sprint over and try to regain possession in an 8v4 game. Players on the outside are allowed to move along the line but are limited to one touch. To score a point, the team in possession must complete ten consecutive passes.

The moment of transition occurs when the four defenders in the middle win back possession. They have to transfer the ball to their teammates in the outside on the other half of the pitch, where the game then becomes an 8v4 again, this time in their favour. Play 3 minute sets and then rotate the inside players with the outside players.

Progressions:

- ✓ Increase the size of the playing area. This now makes it more difficult to win back possession and increases the physical demands on the transitions.

- ✓ Reduce the pass total to six or eight passes for a goal. This should increase the intensity of the exercise as the pressing will have to be more aggressive in order to win the game.

- ✓ On the coach's random call, switch the inside and outside players and restart possession for whatever team transitions quickest. This is another coachable moment for focus and problem solving.

- ✓ Restrict the outside players from passing to another player on the outside. This will give the pressing team an opportunity to 'show' the possession team into an area and increase their chances of winning the ball back.

Coaching Points:

- ✓ The pressing team must have an organization to their pressing. Effective man to man coverage in the middle will make it difficult but it will be tough to win the ball back because of the numerical superiority. Therefore, they will have to take risks.

- ✓ In offensive transition, it may take one or two short passes after winning possession back and attempting to transfer it to the other side of the field. Therefore, players must get in a position for the first pass, or sprint to a position of support for the second pass.

- ✓ Defensive transitions are a huge part of this game. Encourage players to win the ball back immediately after losing it so that it does not get transferred right away.

Exercise Seven

Set-Up:

This exercise takes place in a 30x30 yard area. Teams are split into one team of four (defending team), one team of six (possession team) and two goalkeepers.

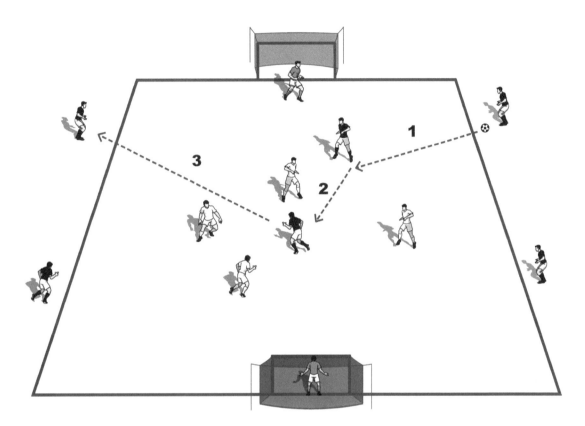

Session Details:

The team in possession (black team) begin the exercise with four players limited to the outside, two players inside, and two goalkeepers. They immediately create an 8v4 situation and aim to work the ball across the field. Every time they transfer the ball from one side to the other, they score a point. The goalkeepers can be used in the transfer but players on the outside cannot switch the play directly from one side to the other.

The goal of the defensive (white) team on the inside is to press the ball with all four players. As soon as they win possession, they can transition immediately and attack either goal. Each game will last two minutes and then rotate the teams and positions.

Progressions:

- ✓ Challenge the players technically on the possession team. Limit the players on the outside to one touch and the players on the inside to two touches.

- ✓ If the possession team make a technical mistake e.g. too many touches or the ball goes out of play, the coach should trigger another ball in quickly to the defensive team. This creates another moment of transition and should challenge players to focus even when the ball is out of play.

- ✓ Add an extra defensive player and now allow players on the outside three touches but only if they 'drive' into the inside with the ball. This will create an additional temporary overload on the inside but will challenge the defensive team to step forward and apply pressure aggressively.

Coaching Points:

- ✓ The defending team are trying to stop the switch, so they must not allow players on the inside to receive the ball sideways on and/or create extra space needed to switch the play. This requires high level of 1v1 defensive skills so you may need to remind defensive players that they must excel at the basics in this exercise.

- ✓ It is important that the defensive team is organized with their pressing. The best solution is to go with a diamond shape and be as compact as they can possibly be.

- ✓ As the goalkeepers can also transfer the ball from one side to the other, make sure they are pressed aggressively and not allowed any "free" passes. Applying pressure here may make the difference between an accurate pass and a wayward one.

- ✓ The game demands a high level of work rate and communication. If, for any reason, those elements are lacking, the quality of defending will drop and the possession team will score easily. If the game moves in that direction or in the opposite one, make sure players understand the relationship between success and energy.

Exercise Eight

Set-Up:

This exercise takes place in a 20x20 yard area. Nine players are split into three teams of three players. Coach will need a supply of balls for quick restarts and to keep intensity levels as high as possible.

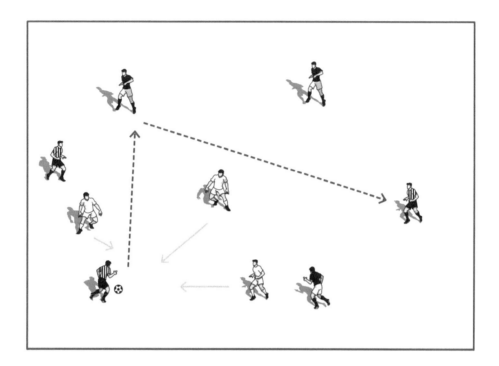

Session Details:

Two teams combine in possession and play against one team, creating a 6v3 game. When the defending team win the ball, the team who gave it away become the new defensive team and the game continues. Players in possession are allowed unlimited touches. Each game lasts 3 minutes, with a one-minute recovery. There are four sets in total.

Progressions:

✓ Introduce a scoring system: If the two teams in possession get ten passes, the defending are awarded a point. After each set, the team with the most points are the losing team.

✓ To increase the technical demands of the exercise, the teams in possession have a two-touch limit.

✓ You can change the structure of the game where now one team is the all-time defending team and must win 5 balls back in total. For every ten passes the teams in possession get, the coach adds an additional ball to the defending team.

Coaching Points:

- ✓ The small sided nature of the game demands that teams can have no passengers defensively. Every player must press and/or stay connected. If one player stops working or slows down significantly, the team will be exposed.

- ✓ Challenge the defensive team to have an organization with their pressing, and then see if they can sustain it.

- ✓ Defensive transitions are a huge part of this game. The reaction of the team who give the ball away should be immediate and positive, because if it is not, the six possession players will make the area as big as possible.

- ✓ The exercise is hard work and physically demanding, so the last thing a team wants to do is give possession straight back after winning it. If this happens under ten seconds continuously, the coach must address offensive transition and identify where it is breaking down for players. It may be technical mistakes, spacing, or decision making.

Exercise Nine

Set-Up:

This exercise takes place in a 20x30 yard area. Twelve players are split into two teams of six, and two goalkeepers are used also. Coach will need a supply of balls for quick restarts and to keep intensity levels as high as possible.

© Copyright www.academysoccercoach.co.uk 2016

Session Details:

Each team occupies one half of the field. The team who starts in possession (white team) have all their players in their half. The defensive team can send four players to aggressively press the ball. If the defending team are successful and win the ball back, they must transfer the ball to their teammates on their half of the field through either A or B gates. Once the ball is transferred through the gates, the teams switch roles and the game continues. However, if they are unsuccessful in transferring the ball through the gates, play restarts in the same half of the field with the same team in possession of the ball. If the team in possession make ten or more passes, they can attempt to score in the goal.

Progressions:

- ✓ Allow the defensive team to use the goalkeeper as an outlet once they win the ball. The goalkeeper can switch the play but must also do it through either A or B gates. This will give the goalkeepers practice at playing under pressure.

- ✓ Remove the gates and now the game should become quicker with a higher level of intensity in transitions.

- ✓ Reduce the number of passes required for a shot on goal. This should result in a higher volume of attacking actions, which should in turn raise competitive levels of the game.

Coaching Points:

- ✓ The defending team have four players at all times and must be organized in their pressing.

- ✓ Once the defending team win the ball back, they are going to require passing options right away. Challenge the defensive players to transition quickly, both physically and mentally, so that they can help their team play out of pressure.

- ✓ Once the possession team make ten passes, challenge the defending team to extend their approach to blocking shots and applying maximum pressure to the player with the ball.

Exercise Ten

Set-Up:

This is a physically demanding, tactical exercise focused around an 11v11 game on a full-sized pitch. The objective of the game is to challenge the teams to transition from possession to pressing at maximum speed and intensity.

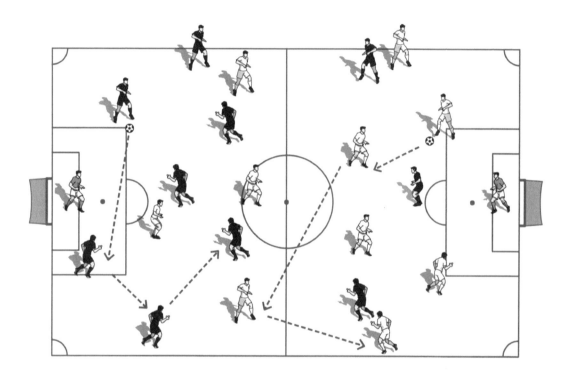

Session Details:

Both teams are organized into their chosen systems. In the above diagram, the white team is in a 4-2-3-1 and the black team is organized into a basic 4-3-3. Before the exercise starts, the coach designates one team as the pressing team (black team above). Both goalkeepers start the exercise simultaneously and team's build-up unopposed. Neither team has a specific pattern of play but the ball is only allowed to go as high as the center forward, before it has to be progressed back to the defensive unit. The only restriction is that players must move in relation to the ball. They are not allowed to remain static in their positioning.

On the coach's signal, the defensive team (black) stop playing their ball and begin to counter-press the white team wherever the ball is at that moment. They have seven seconds to win the ball. If they are successful, they are awarded a point, but if they are not successful, the team in possession is awarded a point. After the press, play starts again from both goalkeepers. This continues for 3 minutes before teams are allowed to recover and then switch roles.

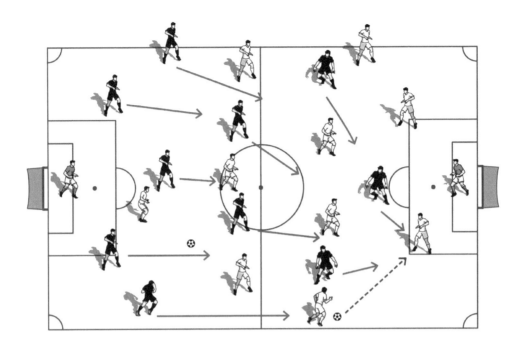

Progressions:

✓ A smaller field will result in more success for the counter-pressing team.

✓ Allow the team in possession to keep playing if they keep possession beyond seven seconds, and award them 3 points for a goal. This now challenges the defensive team to recover after the initial counter-press. Likewise, if the defensive team are successful in winning possession, allow them to continue to play and award them 3 points for a goal.

Coaching Points:

✓ The defensive team will naturally start the exercise quite expansive in their shape. However, they should realize that this makes it difficult to regain the ball back and apply pressure immediately because the spacing is too great. They should then adapt to this by having more short passes in their build-up, becoming more compact, and moving up the field together.

✓ There should be an aggressive reaction from everyone in the defensive team, not just one or two players. If players are not pressing the ball, they must be compressing the field.

✓ The initial goal should be to get 3-5 players around the ball as soon as possible.

✓ How successful is the first player to press? Stress the importance of this player being aggressive without fouling and not allowing the team in possession to progress with the ball.

Summary

✓ Gegenpressing means to pressure the opposition as a collective group immediately after losing the ball.

✓ There are two goals of gegenpressing:
1. Win the ball back as quickly as possible and counter attack.
2. Force the opposition into a rushed or inaccurate pass, which then allows you to gain possession in another area of the field.

✓ You use gegenpressing because:

- Your opponent is most vulnerable when their defensive organization is not established.
- The opposition have just expended energy in their defensive efforts to win the ball.
- You can provide more defensive stability higher up the field if you can press immediately.
- You gain possession of the ball higher up the field, with the possibility of creating a goal-scoring opportunity immediately.
- Today's players are fitter than they have ever been and have the physical ability to press harder and longer than they have ever done before.

✓ There are two dangers to gegenpressing. Firstly, it is a high-risk strategy. Secondly, if one player does not commit to the work, the entire structure collapses.

✓ Before the counter-press, your team must be compact in possession – vertically and laterally.

✓ Player closest to the ball must apply immediate and aggressive pressure. They must not:
  ▪ Dive in
  ▪ Allow penetration
  ▪ Get easily beaten
  ▪ Give away a 'soft' free kick

✓ Rene Maric developed four counter-pressing variants for various coverages:
1. Man-Oriented Gegenpressing
2. Leeway-Oriented Gegenpressing
3. Ball-Oriented Gegenpressing
4. Passing Lane-Oriented Gegenpressing

6
Medium Block

There is a popular misconception of defending today, in my opinion, that organizing numbers behind the ball in a compact manner and inviting the opposition towards you is a negative way of playing and directly conflicts with any attacking philosophy. If we look at it closer however, and study it with a little more depth, we may well find that's not quite the case. Again, with the hype surrounding the game today the media have almost manipulated us into thinking of the game in terms of extremes. Pep Guardiola versus Jose Mourinho have been, without a doubt, the highest profile comparison in recent years. Guardiola has never flinched in his belief of defending from the front, but Mourinho, despite being criticized for constantly imposing a negative approach to his teams has been a little bit more flexible in his approach. Of course, back in 2010, his Inter Milan team produced the ultimate "anti-football" performance as they planted themselves on the edge of the box for the majority of the game and defied the odds as they went on to the Champions League final, at the expense of Barcelona. Mourinho may not have adopted high pressing with his teams in recent years, but that's not to say his teams spend their time in front of their own goal either. The biggest defensive difference between Guardiola and Mourinho is not in which end of the pitch their teams do their work, but instead based around the concept of risk and distances. Quite simply, Guardiola will risk anything and everything to get the ball back immediately, where Mourinho thinks this is unnecessary: if you sit a little further back, the opposition will give it to you sooner rather than later.

In his book 'The Special One: The Dark Side of Jose Mourinho', Spanish journalist Diego Torres summed up Jose Mourinho's attitude to possession at Real Madrid like this:

1. The game is won by the team who commits fewer errors.
2. Football favors whoever provokes more errors in the opposition.
3. Away from home, instead of trying to be superior to the opposition, it's better to encourage their mistakes.
4. Whoever has the ball is more likely to make a mistake.
5. Whoever renounces possession reduces the possibility of making a mistake.
6. Whoever has the ball has fear.
7. Whoever does not have it is therefore stronger.

Although it may sound like the ultimate contradiction to the 'Total Football' philosophy of Guardiola, beneath the surface there are similarities as well as differences. Both believe that simple possession of the ball does not give you a guaranteed advantage. Guardiola has famously attacked tika-taka as misunderstood representation of his playing model. Both coaches also see the opposition having possession as a major opportunity to establish a hold on the game, creating a chance to disrupt the construction of their attack, force mistakes with defensive players out of natural positions, and instil fear from the first moment of the game. It sounds very similar to Jurgen Klopp, who, like Mourinho, has achieved success without a desire to dominate the ball in possession. Therefore, as we study and develop our own system in this book, it is important that we do not get drawn into basic generalizations. There are different ways to defend in different areas, at different stages of the game. Just because we are not pressing the ball high up the pitch, it still is a form of pressing. We are simply implementing it further away from our opponent's goal. Coaches in the modern game must become comfortable with and learn how to infuse different aspects of each defensive system into their own game model, in order to suit the needs of their players and meet the demands of the game.

Which brings us to Diego Simeone. Here is perhaps the best example of a coach who has designed and implemented a system which reflects his coaching philosophy along with the power of his personality. Similar to Pochettino, Simeone is a graduate of the Marcelo Bielsa coaching school, and has created somewhat of a hybrid-defensive system, incorporating a high pressing along with an ultra-aggressive mentality inside a medium block with his Atletico Madrid team. Like Mourinho, he is a believer that defensive teams can take control of the game without the ball.

"Games are not won by those who play well but by those who play safe." In addition, Simeone has proved that 4-4-2 still has value in the modern game. Many have dismissed the efficiency of that particular playing system because of the rise of 3-man central midfields, with coaches reluctant to give up numerical superiority. Simeone however, believes that a team with vertical and horizontal compactness, transitional efficiency, combined with an insatiable desire for work, can easily overcome that challenge. Even though the opposition can advance the ball easily to a point, they struggle to break through the Atletico pressure.

Atletico's defensive mentality is shown in a number of critical areas. Having only conceded 18 goals in the entire 2015/2016 La Liga season, research from StatsBomb.com for the 2015/2016 year concluded that they were also:

1. Toughest to progress the ball into the danger zone against
2. Toughest to actually complete a pass in the danger zone
3. Toughest to carry the ball into the danger zone
4. Toughest to play a short pass to set up a chance against
5. 2nd toughest to get a close shot against
6. Toughest to get a shot clean through on goal against

"I'm not a coach who thinks there is only one way to play, my way is not the only one that counts. I value my players and from them I seek the best way to play together."
Diego Simeone

Why Use a Medium Block?

There are a number of reasons why a team would apply a Medium Block:

- It is almost physically impossible to maintain a high press for every minute of the game. There are times when your team will have to regroup and recover in an effective shape.
- Forces the opposition into less dangerous areas by cutting off the middle of the pitch. This area is usually where the most creative players look to receive the ball and do the most damage.
- Invites teams to commit numbers forward, which leaves them vulnerable in terms of both space and numbers to defend the potential counter attack.
- With less risk involved, the coach can have more control over the player's defensive positioning by having them press only on pre-determined triggers and surrounding them with cover.
- Conserves energy. There can be less ground to cover and players can recover inside the defensive shape. This is crucial when energy is required to break out and counter attack.
- Restricts the opposition higher up the field because there are limited vertical passing options. Time and space are at a premium and opponents have to settle for a backwards or square pass, both of which can be triggers to press.
- With limited space, it becomes very difficult for opposition players to receive the ball on the move. By receiving possession statically, it then allows you to be pressed easier and gives the defending player an advantage.

What You Need

Quick Recovery – Similar to high pressing, you will require players with high fitness levels, levels of concentration, and a willingness to work for each other. The team must take defensive shape within seconds of losing the ball.

Team Discipline – It takes a special type of player to embrace the defensive roles and responsibilities that go along with this system. Attacking players are sometimes reluctant to move closer to their own goal than their opponent's goal. You must have forwards that are willing to work – either by showing defenders into areas or intercepting passes.

Team Strategy – Under the defensive organization in the model of play, the team must understand and have complete clarity on the following concepts:

- ✓ In what specific area do we want to win the ball?
- ✓ What is our first line of pressure and how many players will we send?
- ✓ Do we show inside or outside?
- ✓ What are the triggers to press?
- ✓ How many players are you sending into wide areas?
- ✓ Do our central midfielders step initially and create a space in behind?

Full Backs Who Excel in 1v1 – An effective midfield block typically stays narrow, in order to 'show' the opposition into wide areas. Therefore, you require full backs who are comfortable defending in isolated situations. They also need to be multi-functional by having an understanding and appreciation of distances so that they do not invite a penetrating pass into the space between themselves and the center back.

No space between lines – Attacking players at the elite level are now being trained to play 'between the lines' (receive the ball between the midfield and back four) and can destroy teams given time and space in that area. Defensive back fours and midfield units must therefore work together to prevent those areas from opening up.

Leadership in Central Areas – Players who are willing to organize and communicate tactical information to their team. With compactness being a necessity, they will need to sense when distances between positions, both vertically and horizontally, are getting too big.

Quality in Transition – Once possession is won, the counter attack will not be an option every time. Therefore, it is important that your team can keep it and transition successfully into a period of possession. Again, Atletico Madrid excelled in this area and had pass success average of 78% during the 2015-2016 season.

Pressing Traps – There must be a point where you expect to win possession. These traps can be in wide areas, where full backs and wide midfielders can 'double up' on attackers, or by targeting opposing holding midfielders to aggressively press as soon as they receive possession.

Threat on the Break – Without the speed and ability to counter teams after winning possession, you risk the opposition committing extra numbers to their attack and leaves you susceptible to the counter-press.

Importance of the Weak-Side

One of the biggest differences in coaching a high press and a medium block is the role of the weak side defensive players in advanced positions (wide midfielders and forwards). In a high press, the intense pressure generated on the ball can typically compensate for space on the weak side, but in a medium block that space will be exposed. The breakdown occurs when the weak side player (number 7 on the next page) misinterprets their defensive responsibilities. During defensive exercises, we tend to coach players to establish individual match-ups and then focus on winning them. Because the opponents want to be expansive in possession, the full-back has the potential to drag the wide midfielder out of position, just like in the following example. This creates a problem for the defensive team in central midfield because the #6 and #8 are placed in a very difficult situation. They cannot overcommit to the ball-side because the opponents can easily work the ball into the pocket of space that they just vacated. Likewise, if they do not shift and provide aggressive cover on the ball-side, it will isolate #11 defensively and allow attacking players to receive the ball in half-spaces where they play forward and attack the back four. As coaches, we must focus on the role of the weak side player at all times and make sure players understand exactly where they need to be and, more importantly, why.

© Copyright www.academysoccercoach.co.uk 2017

How to Beat the Block?

As we have discussed earlier in this workbook, no defensive system is bullet proof and the medium block is no different. It is important that we realize where the shortcomings are and then spend time preparing players to deal with them.

1. **Creation of 2v1 Situations** – By spreading the defensive team horizontally or vertically, attacking teams are constantly looking to create and take advantage of numerical advantages, in order to advance the ball and penetrate lines.
2. **Advance the ball quickly in transition** – If attacking teams penetrate upon winning the ball, they will have a higher starting point as a result. This can also remove forward players from contributing to the block.
3. **High tempo passing** –No team can defend the entire width of the field with four or five players. Therefore, when the ball moves quickly in possession, it challenges the defensive players to constantly shift across. This will move the block and spaces open up. Pep Guardiola's teams excel in this alongside his belief that, "The objective is to move the opponent, not the ball."
4. **Combination plays** – A wall pass, overlap, or 3rd man runs can break the defensive lines and create overloads that attacking teams can take advantage of.

5. **Advanced Area Actions** – In his outstanding book, 'The Philosophy of Football: In Shadows of Marcelo Bielsa', Jed Davies explains the value of an attacking player with the ball in between the opposition's midfield and defensive line (see below). Once in this position, attackers can move defenders out of position and exploit the space in behind.

6. **Blindside runs** – One weakness of the medium block is that players have to constantly focus on the ball so they can move and shift accordingly. This invites teams, especially overlapping fullbacks, to attempt advanced runs and penetrate defensive lines and back fours.

7. **Straight Defensive Lines** – If the medium block is simply organized in two straight lines, they can be easily exposed by consecutive forward passes or successful dribbles. Therefore, the defensive team must have a number of defensive layers within their structure to provide balance and cover.

8. **Diagonal passes that break lines** – When half spaces do open up against compact teams, midfielders who can disguise a forward pass become incredibly valuable. Sergio Busquets is a great example of this.

9. **Lapses in concentration** – If one player is out of position or 'switches off' as the attacking team rotates possession, good teams will take advantage. That is sometimes the reason why teams constantly circulate possession against the medium block.

10. **Get numbers in dangerous and unexpected positions** – Under Guardiola, Bayern sometimes overloaded players in non-traditional positions inside attacking zones. Again, this forces the medium block to constantly move around and shift positions, and eventually space can open up. Alternatively, if a team plays without a traditional center forward, it removes the reference point for the defensive line and can cause confusion amongst central defensive pairings. Spain used this tactic to devastating effect during the 2012 European Championships.

11. **Opposite movement of forwards.** (See below) The center forward in white (number 9) makes a run and the center back reacts by tracking it. This movement then opens up space for another attacker (number 7) to move into and receive a pass on the move. With the covering right back out of position, the attacker can now drive into the space left by the center back and create a 1v1 or a 2v1 on the edge of the penalty area.

Exercise One

Set-Up:

This is an exercise designed to work on a team shifting across as units and preventing penetrating passes. The exercise takes place in a 20x20 yard area, split into four zones. Two teams of eight players are organized into two teams of four.

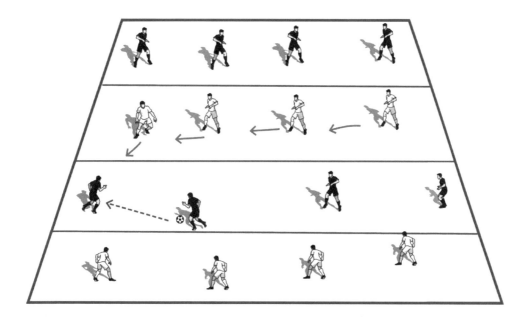

Session Details:

The ball starts in the middle with either team in possession (black team above). If the team in possession can split the defensive line and pass to their teammates in another zone, they are awarded one point. The game then continues and the defensive line must turn around to prevent another point being scored. Defensively, you must stay in your zone and you win possession back by either intercepting a pass or if an opponent fails to control the ball and it goes out of play. The game should move quickly with fast restarts and the first team to ten wins. The units then switch positions and another game resumes.

Progressions:

✓ Players in possession are limited to two touches.

✓ Introduce a limit of four passes so that the team in possession must play a forward pass quicker and avoids the game turning into a possession exercise.

✓ One defensive player can go into the opponents' zone at a time.

Coaching Points:

✓ As the ball travels across the zone, so too must the defensive line.

✓ When the first defensive player steps forward to get as close to the ball as possible, the second defender must cover in behind so that they do not get split with one pass.

✓ Transitional moments are very important in this game so if a team splits a defensive line with a pass, the defending players must re-organize themselves immediately so that they do not lose another point right away.

Exercise Two

Set-Up:

This exercise is from Diego Simeone and his Atletico Madrid team and is similar to Exercise One in terms of the defensive shape and movement patterns. Where it differs however, is the individual accountability of each defensive player and the reaction to the penetrating pass if it is completed. The field is 20x20 yards, split vertically into four zones. Twelve players are organized into two teams, with four defensive players in each zone and then two attacking players behind the opposing team and close to the goal.

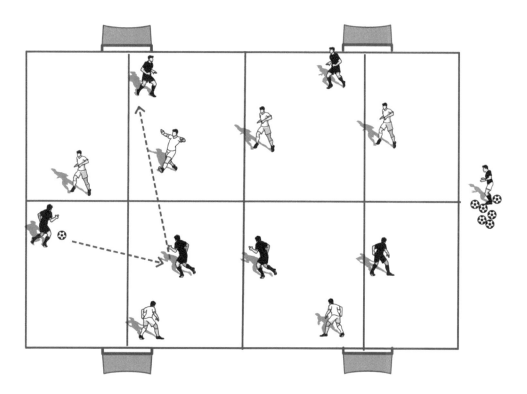

Session Details:

Coach can start the exercise by playing to either team. The goal is to find a penetrating pass, which splits the defensive line and finds one of the attacking players on the other side. The attacking players have two touches and must finish in one of the mini goals. Defensively, the players must stay in their own zone and therefore must shift over as a unit to prevent forward passes. Once a pass is intercepted, the exercise then continues with the defensive team in possession. If a forward pass is played to one of the attackers, the defending team can 'collapse' and apply pressure immediately in order to prevent the goal being scored. The coach restarts the game quickly and the first team to 10 goals wins the game.

Progressions:

- ✓ Limit the players to two touches so that the ball moves quickly.

- ✓ Introduce a limit of four passes so that the team in possession must play a forward pass quicker and avoids the game turning into a possession exercise.

- ✓ Restrict the attacking players to one touch and they must combine to score. In other words, one must lay-off the ball for the other. This challenges the attacking players to work together and also the defensive team to react to both players once a forward pass is completed.

Coaching Points:

- ✓ When the ball goes into a zone:
    - o Defensive player must step forward to the line and attempt to apply pressure immediately.
    - o All three remaining defensive players must get to the edge of their zones and drop off slightly so that they can intercept the pass.
    - o If the ball is transferred to another zone, this 'piston-like' action continues.

- ✓ As the coach restarts the exercise quickly, the defensive team must quickly re-organize themselves. Constant communication helps with roles and responsibilities, as well as keeping the tempo high.

- ✓ If a forward pass is completed, every defensive player must react immediately and work to prevent the goal. No player should be standing watching.

Exercise Three:

Set-Up:

This is an exercise that can be used as a warm-up or a cool-down. It reinforces shape and positioning, as well as establishing distances and areas of cover. There is also a certain amount of flexibility for coaches in terms of organization. Players can work in specific units or blocks of time. Coaches can then make this as intense or physically demanding as they choose to.

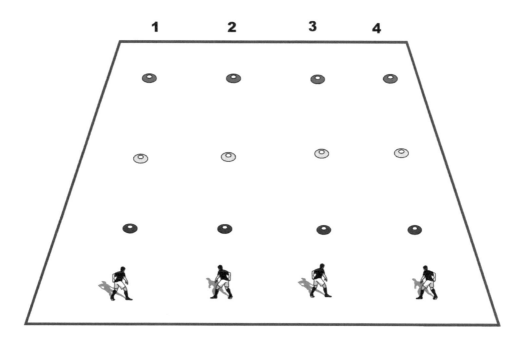

Session Details:

Players start in groups of four with three different colored cones positioned directly ahead of each one. The coach starts the exercise by calling out a number and color, which have all been identified to the players. When the coach calls out a number and color, the players have five seconds to react and take up the correct positions: The initial player must get as close as possible to the cone, with the other three players taking up compact covering positions. The players then have five seconds to recover back to their starting positions, before the coach calls another color and number.

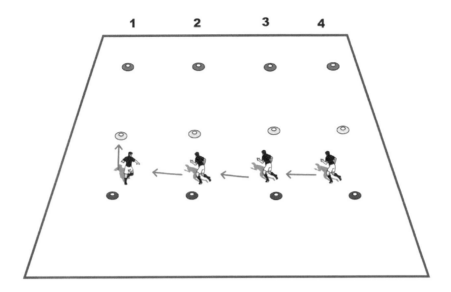

Progressions:

✓ Again, the coach can manipulate the exercise to increase distances and times. They can also adapt the shape of the covering players towards their own system.

✓ Add five opposition players and two min-goals (See below). The objective of the defensive team (in black) is now to apply their shape and pressure in a small-sided game. The possession team score by dribbling into the End Zone. Attacking players cannot receive the ball inside the End Zone. If the defensive team win the ball, they can counter by scoring in either of the mini-goals.

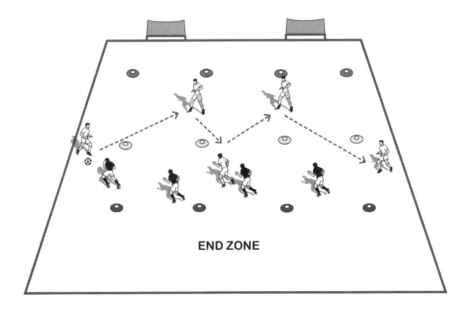

END ZONE

Coaching Points:

✓ The initial player must get to the first cone with speed and intent.

✓ Supporting players must use their body shape to 'show' play into the area that the team wants to show.

✓ Challenge the players to recover quickly and keep intensity levels high. If speed leaves the exercise, the focus levels of the players will vanish as well.

Exercise Four

Set-Up:

This game is designed for attacking teams to attempt to expose their opponents in wide areas and also leave them vulnerable to spaces in the middle, as well as the ball being switched quickly. Two teams of seven players with one goalkeeper are organized into three defenders and four midfielders.

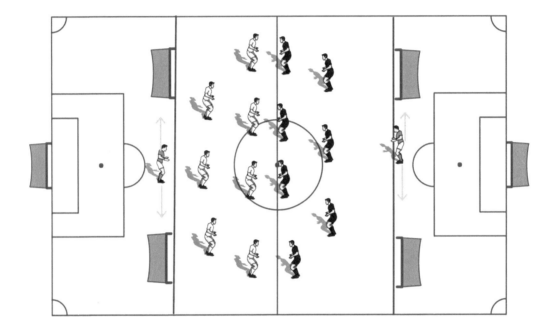

Session Details:

Play starts with an 8v8 game, with both teams having an option of scoring in two goals. It is physically challenging for goalkeepers too, as they must cover both goals. In possession there are no limitations, as players are free to move and can shoot from anywhere. Defensively, teams must establish initial shape and then prevent their opponents from attacking in wide areas. Play 4x4 minute games with a one-minute recovery in between.

Progressions:

✓ The game is designed initially for both sides to cancel each other out in terms of team shape. However, to progress the game and challenge the players tactically, the coach can organize the teams into different systems and see how they react.

✓ Add a forward who can only operate on the line between both goals and is limited to one or two touches. This will challenge defensive teams to stop a penetrating pass through the middle and then react quickly if it does happen.

Coaching Points:

✓ The shape in this example is designed to overload players in their defensive roles. For example, a defensive-3 will have to be aggressive in their shifting and cannot have a spare player on the weak side. Likewise, because the midfield will have offensive roles, they will also find the exercise physically demanding.

✓ Because the goals are in wide areas and with a goalkeeper, players must excel in 1v1 defending and attempt to provide cover immediately.

✓ Body shape is also critical in 1v1 defending. Encourage players to stop the switch as that is where they are vulnerable.

✓ If a player is out of position in transition, the defensive team must solve the problem accordingly. Pressure must be applied to the ball.

Exercise Five

Set-Up:

This exercise focuses on the transition from attack to defense and challenges players physically to cover long distances and recover defensive shape. It is designed for both wide and central attacking players and works best with at least three groups (12 players or more) so that work to rest ratios are adequate.

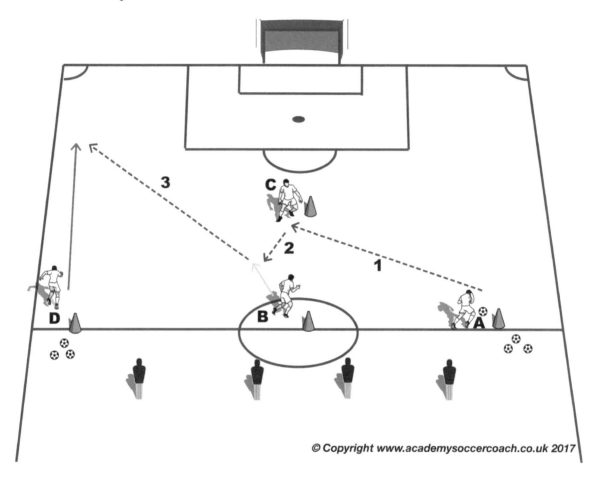

© Copyright www.academysoccercoach.co.uk 2017

Session Details:

Four players begin on the starting cones above. Players A and D are wide attackers, with C and B central attackers. The exercise begins with a pattern play to goal. As the ball is worked out to Player D, the other three players in the build-up should attack the penalty area and get in position to finish the cross delivered from the wide player. Because this is unopposed, you can give the four players a time limit for completion (e.g. 8-10 seconds). Immediately after the attack has finished, the four players have 10 seconds to sprint back to their mannequin (next page), where they can recover in their defensive shape.

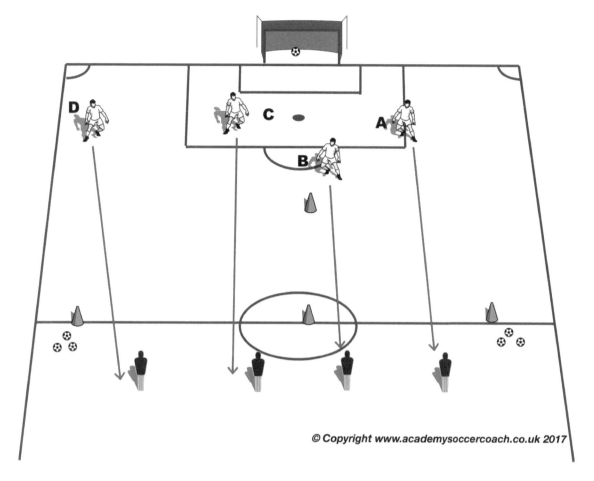

© Copyright www.academysoccercoach.co.uk 2017

Progressions:

✓ Coach can manipulate the times, both in the attack and the recovery, to increase or decrease the physical demands of the exercise.

✓ Add three defenders and give A, B, C, and D the freedom to attack in any way they like. Keep the time limit to avoid it turning into a possession exercise.

✓ Have 3-4 attacking units and have them compete against each other. Award one point for a goal and deduct points if every player does not recover in time.

✓ You can adapt the resting positions to suit your specific tactical model.

Coaching Points:

✓ It is important that the work rate and quality is high during the attack phase of the exercise because you want it to match the intensity of the game.

✓ Many players struggle in transition inside their attacking third and would rather recover, and then work themselves back. In this exercise, we are encouraging players to work back first, and then recover in position. Players must recognize the difference.

✓ Explain how the recovery position is related to the medium block and this is the position the players will be required to work back to during the game.

Exercise Six

Set-Up:

This exercise focuses on pressing the ball from inside a compact shape. The goal is to avoid spaces for midfielders to play forward. It is played as an 11v11 game from the edge of both penalty areas. The field is divided into thirds and there is a 5x5 yard box for each goalkeeper.

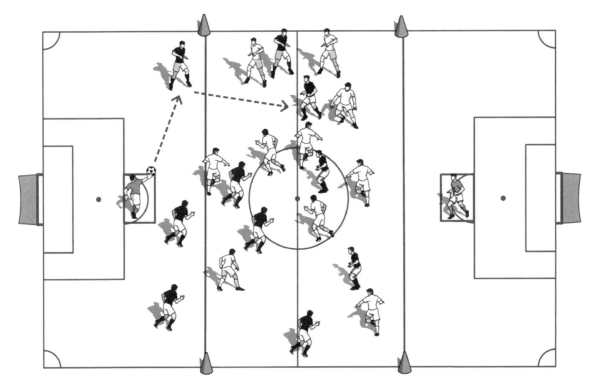

© Copyright www.academysoccercoach.co.uk 2016

Session Details:

Both teams are set up in an organized system, with players given specific roles. The game always starts from the goalkeeper and the objective of the team in possession is to play a lofted pass to the opposing goalkeeper inside their box. If team in possession find the opposing goalkeeper from their defensive third, they are awarded three points. If they find the opposing goalkeeper from in the middle third they are awarded two points, and if they do it inside the attacking third, they are awarded one point. The scoring system challenges the players to always maintain pressure on the ball at every stage of the field. If the opposing team win the ball, the same rules apply. Each game should last six minutes long.

Progression:

- ✓ Make the field full size, remove the 5x5 yard boxes for keepers and now allow them to move anywhere inside their penalty area. Although the distances are bigger, the movement of the goalkeeper will challenge teams to maintain their high pressing standards.

Coaching Points:

- ✓ Defensively, the pressing must be ultra-aggressive because the goal is to prevent long passes, rather than shots on goal. Therefore, players must constantly be aware of distances in supporting roles and in closing down the ball.

- ✓ Although aggressive pressure is required, so too is discipline. If a pressuring player dives in and is beaten easily, it will most likely cost his/her team points.

- ✓ Concentration levels must remain high as teams will have the ability to score from wide areas also. Many teams in possession will attempt to solve the spacing problem by drifting into wide areas, so defensively players need to be aware of this and constantly communicate with one another.

- ✓ If a team presses aggressively in the middle third and fails to win possession, how quickly can they recover if the team in possession advances the ball into the final third. Teams must understand that the goal is to prevent points in all areas of the field, so must also excel in the recovery aspect.

Exercise Seven

Set-Up:

This is an 8v10 game that works on the defensive team's shape from an opponent's attack in a central area. The defensive team (white) are organized numerically and are set-up without a center forward (number 9).

Session Details:

The defensive team start the exercise inside their own half in a 4-2-3 system, with their attacking midfielder (number 10) on the end-line with the server. The black team are organized into a 4-1-3. The server triggers the start of the exercise by playing the ball into one of the central midfielders. As soon as the ball is played, the white team must react quickly. The number 10 must work their way back into position and press the ball from behind. The goal of the attacking team is to play through the pressure and score in the goal. If the defending team are successful in winning possession, they are awarded one point for dribbling over the end-line with the ball under control. This would simulate a counter attack in a real game. After the attack is finished, both teams are given 10 seconds to recover into their starting positions, before the next ball is played. Each set should last for at least 4 minutes in order to test the players physically, as well as tactically.

Progressions:

- ✓ Add more players to the attacking team gradually, where eventually you work into an overload in their favour.

- ✓ Decrease the recovery time so that the transitions become quicker and challenge the defensive team to re-organize immediately, as well as testing players under fatigue.

- ✓ Introduce a number 9 to the defensive team and open the exercise up to an 11v11 game on a full field.

Coaching Points:

- ✓ Number 10 presses from the weak side.

- ✓ Number 6 steps forward to apply pressure, with number 8 providing cover.

- ✓ Numbers 7 and 11 move inside to cover the numbers 6 and 8, as well as 'showing' the opposition into a wide area.

- ✓ Back four (numbers 2, 3, 4 and 5) step up to compact the area, become compact (both horizontally and vertically), and have a 'sideways on' body shape to deal with potential long balls over the defensive line.

- ✓ If the ball goes into a forward player, the defenders should not allow them to turn and the midfielders should collapse their shape immediately to compress the area.

- ✓ Once the ball goes into a wide player, pressure should be applied immediately by the closest midfielder or fullback, and they should try to keep the attacking team playing down one side.

Summary

✓ The pressing game is not black and white. Just because you do not high press, it does not mean that you are a negative or defensive-minded coach.

✓ Klopp, Simeone, Guardiola, and Mourinho all look at the opposition having possession as an opportunity. The difference between them is centered around risks and distances.

✓ Benefits of a medium block include that it cuts off the middle of the pitch, reduces space for attacking players in between lines, reduces physical demands, offers a threat on the counter attack, and limits attacking players to receiving the ball into their feet.

✓ To successfully implement a medium block, you will require high levels of recovery, team discipline, collective understanding of individual roles and responsibilities, full backs who are strong defenders, limited spaces between defensive and midfield lines, leadership, effective transitions, pressing traps, and a threat on the break.

✓ The block can be beaten by creation of overloads, high tempo passing, advanced area actions, blindside runs, straight defensive lines, lapses in concentration, non-traditional attacking positions, and opposite movement of forwards.

7
High Pressing

When the great Johan Cruyff said, "Playing football is very simple, but playing simple football is the hardest thing there is," I'm almost convinced that he was referring to pressing. When you observe it from afar the principles can seem relatively simple: run, work hard, close down space, and be aggressive. But when we peel back the layers, however, it becomes more and more complex. In this book, we have previously addressed the decision making and individual intricacies of pressing. Now comes the ultimate test for the press – performing it against top-class opposition. The higher the level, the more problems you will be presented with and the increased likelihood of your defensive shape getting exposed. No team or coach who presses gets through unscathed. You cannot avoid it, but you can prepare for it. Our work in this chapter now looks at how to prepare extensively against a variety of playing systems and how the opposition influences our defensive positioning and traps, as well as how they can break the press.

Starting Positions

"Don't mark a player, cover the space between two players. The opponent thinks he's unmarked, making pressing easier" – Pep Guardiola

Players must understand that their positioning prior to the press, can dictate whether they actually get an opportunity to implement it at all. Inviting the press is all about an appreciation of distances and the discipline to commit to without giving into the temptation of tight marking. Below we can see that, when the opposition goalkeeper has the ball, all the forwards in the white team have man-marked their direct opponents. While this may give the impression of applying pressure high up the pitch, it actually discourages even the best possession teams from building their attack. Presented with this picture, the goalkeeper will likely opt for a long, lofted pass over the press and the attackers will have to recover in defensive positions as the 50-50 ball is contested in midfield. In addition, initial man-marking can also let an opponent in behind them with space to receive.

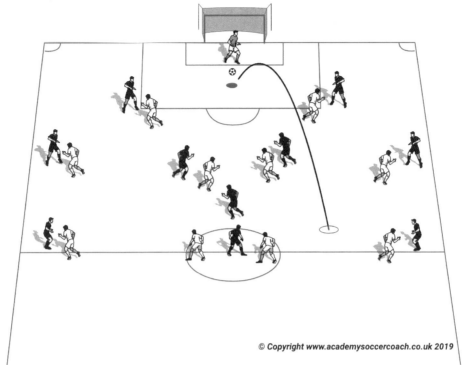

Below you can see how the distances before the press can change the picture significantly. By covering the space in-between players, as opposed to man-marking, the white team are not only inviting the ball to be played into areas where they can apply pressure, they can also send multiple players within short distances and create a numerical superiority. These principles are important when we are designing high-press practices and we must challenge players to consistently make positional judgements, rather than have fixed starting points to begin a pressing practice. Like every aspect of pressing, the decision-making process of creating effective starting points must be practised both individually and as a team.

Pressing Against Direct Opponents

Recent studies have shown that the game is becoming more and more compact with less space on the field and time on the ball. Because of this, the number of explosive actions (sprints, duels, etc.) has increased by 40% over the last 8-10 years. When a pressing team goes head-to-head with an opponent who has a direct style of play, this trend is exemplified. The nature of the game becomes fast and furious with both teams trying to establish their defensive game first and focus primarily on winning the physical battle. Because of this, the direct team take few risks in the build-up phase and opt to go over the pressure. This results in more long passes, aerial duels, second balls, and counter pressing. The US college game has come under fire for providing a similar game template of constant 'pressing, long balls, and knock downs'. Quality in possession can be in short supply but the reality is that it happens in the professional game too, albeit not quite with the same frequency.

Why has the Guardiola pressing style struggled in its first year in England? There could be a number of tactical and personnel reasons but a major area where City have struggled is in these explosive defensive actions. In Spain, for example, when his Barcelona team press, opposition teams are built on possession models and therefore try to play through or around the press. In England, however, teams tend to take less risks. As of January 16, 2017, City had only won 33% of their tackles, which is the worst record in the Premier League. When Guardiola took his talented team to the most direct, counter-attacking team in the league, Leicester City, they found themselves three goals down after just twenty minutes. He has been dismissive of working on this aspect of the game, "'I'm not coaching tackles. I'm not training for tackles … what's tackles?'" Instead it may impact his recruitment over the next two years and it will be interesting to see if Guardiola brings a more combative player to Manchester City and looks to strengthen in this area.

Another dynamic of pressing against a direct system of play is the impact it has on defensive line positioning. A pressing team will obviously look to get their defensive line high up the field once they initiate the press. As their opponents look to go long with their passing options, the back line is vulnerable with space in behind. In addition, a direct team will usually have pace up front. Speed of course plays a huge role in the solution, but so too does starting positions and body shape. The defenders must be sideways on, avoid being caught flat footed and read the situation early so they can give themselves a head start on the forward. (See below)

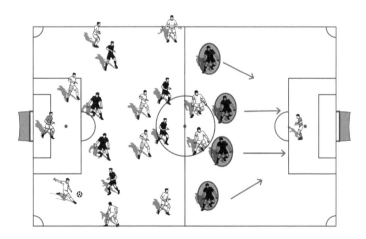

Different Systems, Different Solutions

"Football is not just about players. It is about shape and about space, about the intelligent deployment of players, and their movement within that deployment." (Jonathan Wilson, Inverting the Pyramid)

Ultimately, there is no right or wrong system to press against another. Everyone is equipped with its advantages and disadvantages, there are always a number of variables to consider like quality of opposition, age group, etc. Although no formation is bullet proof, coaches today must understand the pictures that will develop and learn how to take advantage of tactical opportunities that will be presented. The higher the level, the more preparation is required in scouting and anticipating specific tendencies in both teams and individuals. For coaches without the luxury of a scouting network or a match analysis department, you can still prepare for most teams and anticipate potential scenarios. Today's game sees a majority of back fours, with full-backs high and wide, and a central rotation of three midfielders, including one holder. It is important to remember that the objective is to invite the opposition to play in an area where either they are weak or you are strong.

Pressing in a Traditional 4-3-3

"Anticipate what your opponent will do (and what you can do), it will put us closer to victory… this is my aim as a coach! When I was a player I asked the coach to anticipate as much as possible of what was going to happen in the game and prevent insecurity, fear, and doubts." Pep Guardiola

The goal of pressing in this system is to filter possession to the outside (full-backs) and then apply aggressive pressure from the forward line. Once the ball goes into a wide area, the team will shift across and then compress the play horizontally. Stopping the switch is a critical part of this system because the defensive team will have overloaded on the strong side and they are vulnerable on the weak side. This system can provide multiple lines of cover and if the wide midfielders are successful in winning possession, there is the possibility of a 3v2 counter attacking opportunity.

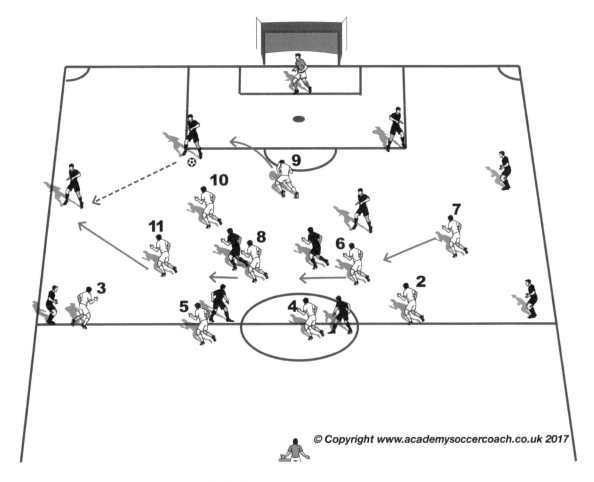

© Copyright www.academysoccercoach.co.uk 2017

Positional Roles and Responsibilities

#9 – Curves their run to avoid the switch of play and then applies pressure to the center back who has the ball. They must always block the return pass if the center back finds a full-back or the holder.

#10 – Cuts off and presses the passing lane into the holding midfielder. By preventing the ball into the holder, you also prevent another way for the possession team to switch the play.

#6 and #8 – The strong side player works to cover the #10 and possibly pick up the opposition midfielder if they drift higher up the pitch. The weak side player shifts over and provides cover.

#11 – Stays central initially and presses if the center back progresses the ball to their side. If not, they sit off the full back and invite the pass (which adds another trigger to press aggressively)

#7 – Tucks in to help keep the shape horizontally compact and adds an extra number in midfield. They should also be in a position to apply pressure immediately if the press is broken and the ball is switched to the opposite full-back.

#GK – Plays high off their line in order to read the ball over the top.

Remaining players – Shift over to get compact and create a strong side. Back four will step up to the halfway line and compress the space in front.

Pressing in a Traditional 4-4-2

Initial positioning within this system is about compactness and cover. Again, the goal is typically to filter the play towards the outside and then set a pressing trap. It also offers an opportunity to apply aggressive pressure to both center backs when they are in possession of the ball. There should be limited space in between defensive lines so it is crucial that the defensive team constantly moves together in relation to the ball.

© Copyright www.academysoccercoach.co.uk 2017

<u>Positional Roles and Responsibilities</u>

#9 and #10 – Forwards work off one another. The one closest to the ball applies aggressive pressure (#10 above) and forces them to play down one side. The other forward has a decision to make: If the passing lane to the other center back is open, they must stay high and close it off. Alternatively, if the first forward forces the center back to play down one side, they must then drop in and be prepared to mark or double team the holding midfielder.

#6 and #8 – The strong side player works to cover the #10 and possibly pick up the opposition midfielder if they drift higher up the pitch. The weak side player shifts over and provides cover.

#11 – Stays central to invite the pass to the full-back. This adds the trigger to press aggressively. Also, if #9 or #10 has put the center back under immense pressure, they can push up, assist in the press, and offer an attacking option once the ball is won.

#7 – Tucks in to help keep the shape horizontally compact. If the opposition circulate the ball quickly and open up space in the central midfield area, they may have to step in and provide cover. Alternatively, if the ball is worked to the opposite full-back, they go out and press immediately.

#3 and #2 – The strong side player must keep shape centrally when the ball is with the opposition center back. Then, once the ball is played to the full-back, close down the space and take away the passing option to the advanced wide player. This will help create the pressing trap. The weak side player remains connected with the center backs and provides cover if the ball is progressed into the forward line.

#4 and #5 – Step up to the halfway line and compress the space behind the midfield line to allow them to step. If the ball is played into a wide area, step over to get compact and create a strong side.

#GK – Plays high off their line in order to read the ball over the top.

Pressing in a 4-4-2 Diamond Against a 3-5-2

The difference with the diamond pressing is that the pressing trap is now in the center of the pitch, with the numerical advantage in that zone. The vulnerabilities of the system lie in wide areas, therefore, passing lanes from the opposing center backs to outside backs must be blocked as this will move. The goal with this pressing system is to press on the second pass and then capitalize on the break in a central area. Again, this is another system where you can have multiple lines of cover.

Positional Roles and Responsibilities

#9 and #10 – Curve their runs and cut off the passing lane to the outside defenders. They work together to pressure the central defender sideways on and 'show' them into the middle where the pressing trap awaits.

#6 and #8 – Depending on what the opposition do, one will take care of the deep lying holder while the other will pick up the attacking option further up the field. When the center back is driving forward, they should be 'touch-tight' and in a position where they can either stop service or win the ball back.

#11 and #7 – Initially stay central and cut off the passing lane between the central midfielder and wing-backs. They must also take a position that allows them to pressure immediately if the ball is played into the middle.

#2 and #3 – If the white team are successful in working the ball wide to either wing-backs, both #2 and #3 must be in a position where they can either apply immediate pressure, or cover for their wide midfielders. If the wing-backs are given time and space, they can attack the back four and the press is compromised.

#4 and #5 - Create a compact midfield by squeezing and applying a high line. They must constantly communicate shape and positioning with the fullbacks and midfielders.

#GK – Plays high off their line in order to read the ball over the top.

High Press Killers

Ultra-Aggressive Approach – As we addressed earlier in this workbook, the entire defensive pressing structure can collapse if one player does not fulfil his/her roles. For many attacking players, individual 1v1 defending is typically a weakness in their game. They have not practised defensive principles and typically bypass the art of delay and slowing down on approach. Quite often, this leads to a forward 'bailing out' defensive player by fouling or overcommitting to the challenge.

Reactors vs. Readers – There are two types of players in a high pressing system. There are those who can interpret cues and see potential situations develop (Readers). Then there are those players who wait and respond to everything the opposition is doing (Reactors). Against good teams, you need a lot more 'Readers' than 'Reactors', especially with space constantly being vacated in potentially dangerous areas for opposing players.

Consecutive Forward Passes - Although one forward pass can play into a pre-planned pressing trap, two consecutive ones typically destroy it. This usually occurs when a team is disorganized in their press, with only one single line of pressure, and lack support structures in place. Space is then created between the defensive and midfield units. For example, a forward player has created a pressing opportunity, but a midfielder suffers a tactical breakdown and an opposition player is then presented with time and space to destroy the defensive shape.

Free Turns – Ironically, many times a well-executed team press is ruined by a defender making a decision-making error high up the field. Away from their own goal and without cover, defenders are sometimes more reluctant than attackers to apply aggressive pressure as they fear they will be exposed if they are not successful. The worst thing they can do, however, is stand off and allow an attacking player to turn and expose the press as it collapses.

Lack of Communication – With so many triggers and the pictures constantly changing, it is almost impossible for a coach to manage and conduct every pressing action throughout a game. A pressing team must have players who are constantly passing on information to one another and reminding each other of roles and responsibilities. A quiet team typically lacks energy and leadership; two essential ingredients for a pressing team.

Ball Playing Center Backs – As forwards press defenders who are less comfortable in possession, the future elite center backs will be required to break pressure themselves. David Luiz already excels in this and has given Chelsea an extra dimension in the 2016/2017 season as they build out of the back. In the near future, coaches may have to decide which defender they press and which ones they give extra consideration to.

Triggers

It is physically impossible to press every single opportunity; therefore, teams must identify moments in the game where they can press as a team. It keeps everyone on the same page and develops an understanding of the defensive system. Jed Davies has studied pressing in the modern game for a number of years. His research has found that, at Southampton, Mauricio Pochettino had fifteen pressing triggers for his players. Now that is a complex system! With the understanding that not all coaches are working with Premier League professionals, Davies looked to simplify this and broke pressing triggers down to four main categories.

1. **Attacking team are not yet organized/ yet to transition into a shape that supports ball retention.** This is a really aggressive reaction to losing possession and there are a variety of ways to do it. Barcelona caused havoc with their '6 Second Rule' on the rare occasions that possession was given away. Another way is that if the defenders outnumber the attackers or a 1v1 situation.

2. **Opponent's conditions for control are not present or are yet to be created**. This is an opportunity to press that is caused by favourable circumstances for the defensive team, such as a bad pitch, a bouncing ball, a slow pass, a backwards pass, or when an opponent receives the ball under uncomfortable conditions, i.e. on their weaker foot or with a square body shape.

3. **Patterned traps**. A number of top teams force the ball wide and then set about pressing aggressively. This is because space is at a premium and teams in possession only have one direction in which to play out. Pep Guardiola once famously stated, "The touchline is the best defender in the world." His Barcelona and Bayern Munich teams have excelled in showing teams into wide areas and pouncing on them.

4. **Pressure in relation to risk.** Davies believes that teams who press high up the pitch have three different approaches, depending on what area the moment occurs. These are man-to-man pressing, zonal pressing, and option-based pressing. Man-to-man typically follows the rule of 'nearest man' closing the opponent down and forcing them to play a long ball out of pressure. Zonal pressing is when pressing teams force play into a defensively overloaded area and usually takes place around the midfield area. Option-based pressing forces play into a predictable area, only for players to act quickly upon the pass into the only option left open and is often the basis for setting traps in different areas of the field.

Exercise One

Set-Up:

This exercise is designed to implement and develop a system where the coach wants forwards and/or midfielders to press the ball high in a 4-3-3 and prevent possession through the midfield. It also challenges players in 1v1 defensive situations, with little or no cover. It takes place on one half of the field with two mini-goals across the middle, facing the sidelines. Twelve players are used including a goalkeeper. The black team is organized with a goalkeeper, a back four, and two central midfielders and the white team has two midfielders and three forwards.

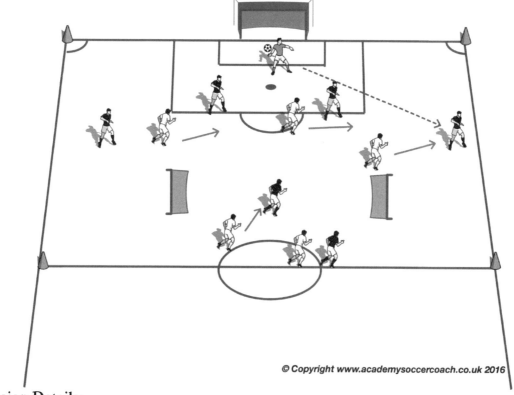

Session Details:

Before you begin, hold the starting positions of the three forwards in white further back so that they must get into position quickly to start the press. The exercise starts from the goalkeeper, who must play short to a defender. The defenders (black) have an initial 4v3 advantage to build up from. The goal of the team in possession is to pass into one of the mini-goals facing outwards. They do this with as many or as few passes as they choose. If the white team press the ball and win possession, they can counter on the other goal.

Progressions:

  ✓ Change the system of play for both sides. This can be done in order to cater the exercise to your own system, to educate your players on different styles of pressing, or to increase the physical demands for players.

  ✓ Create a 3v2 overload in the central area where the team in possession now have someone who can change the point of attack and make the game much more difficult for the pressing team.

Coaching Points:

✓ The forwards must make sure they work together to press the back four and do not allow the possession team time and space to progress the ball. Therefore, they must be organized and work together.

✓ Individually, the forwards must 'show' the defenders wide and then keep them there. This will require a lot of discipline and commitment, but should also reduce options for the player in possession and thus increase their chances of winning the ball.

✓ Defensive midfielders must realize that the forwards are probably going to overcommit strong side and leave the weak side exposed. Because of this, they must prevent the opposition midfield from switching the point of attack.

✓ If the defensive team are successful in winning possession, they will eventually be outnumbered so it may be better to penetrate in under four passes rather than opt for possession.

Exercise Two

Set-Up:

This is a highly competitive exercise that challenges the defensive team to apply aggressive pressure against a back four and midfield who initially have to possess, but are then given an outlet to break the press and score. The game takes place on one half of the field, with three mini-goals located at the halfway line. Fourteen players are used in total, including a goalkeeper.

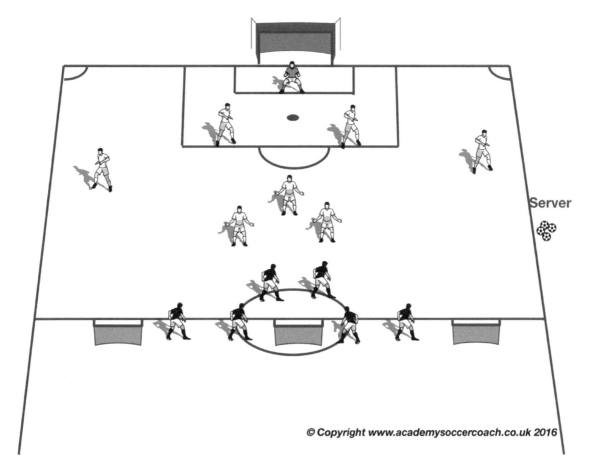

© Copyright www.academysoccercoach.co.uk 2016

Session Details:

One team (white) is organized with a goalkeeper, back four, and a midfield three – who take up their positions before the exercise starts. The opposition (black team) will be the pressing team and are organized into two center forwards and four midfielders. They start the exercise on the halfway line, with the two forwards allowed to advance to the edge of the circle. The coach starts the exercise by playing a long pass to the goalkeeper. This is the trigger for the defensive team to begin the press and start their defensive movements. The goalkeeper can immediately play any fullback, who must complete one pass before the white team can score in any of the three goals. The pressing team are trying to aggressively win the ball and then counter in the main goal. After the ball goes out of play, both sets of players must recover to their starting positions. The coach can manipulate the physical demands of the exercise by having two groups who alternate, or working with one group and including a rest period.

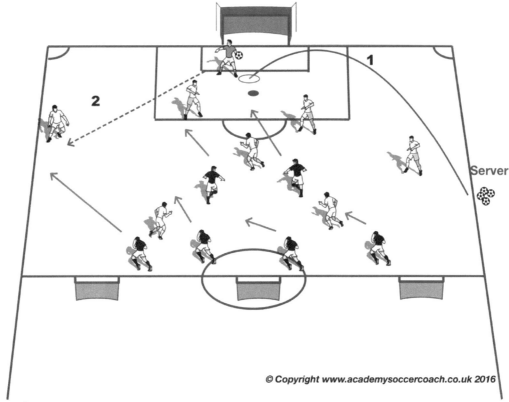

Progression:

✓ Remove the one pass restriction on the fullbacks and now the wide pressing players must get there even quicker to take away the immediate scoring option.

✓ Allow the goalkeepers to play either center back or holding midfielder and see how this changes the defensive organization of the pressing team.

✓ After the ball goes out of play, immediately restart the game with a ball to the black team. It now becomes a two-ball exercise and you can challenge the pressing team on transitioning offensively also.

✓ You can change the shape and consequently the numbers of the exercise, depending on what your system is and/or who you will be playing against.

Coaching Points:

✓ Although this is an aggressive, high pressing transition game, the key is in the organization, as well as the physical output of the pressing team. Make sure every player is aware of the roles and responsibilities they have in their position.

✓ The ball from the coach is designed as a visual cue to get the pressing team high up the field immediately. It may come in a game from a back pass or a defensive clearance from the pressing team.

✓ 1v1 defending is critical in this game because if any defender or midfielder on the wide team creates space on or off the ball, they are potentially in a scoring opportunity. Keep reminding players of those individual defensive principles.

Exercise Three

Set-Up:

This is a physically demanding exercise that challenges teams to press aggressively high up the field and prevent both short and long passes. The game takes place on one half of the field with sixteen players used in total. The white team is organized with a back four and a midfield three, whereas the black team is organized with a midfield three and three forwards. There is also a goalkeeper and two target players, located at gates A and B.

© Copyright www.academysoccercoach.co.uk 2016

Session Details:

The exercise begins from the goalkeeper. The coach can start players further up the field to make the exercise realistic. The goalkeeper must play short to any defender and this is the trigger for the press from the forwards and midfield on the black team. The goal of the white team in possession is to play the ball to either target player at A or B. This wins the possession team a point. If a point is scored, however, a transition element arrives as the target players immediately play to the black team who can then attack the goal. The possession team (white) then becomes the defensive team and the black team are then challenged in offensive transition. The game lasts 4 minutes in total with a one-minute recovery. Midfielders and target players should change after every game.

Progressions:

- ✓ If the white team complete six or more passes, they also score a point. This will add another degree of urgency to the pressing.

- ✓ Put the target players at A and B on the defensive (black) team. Now, when a goal is scored from the possession team, the black team are transitioning with two extra players. Does this change their decision in the transition phase, i.e. possession versus counter attack?

Coaching Points:

- ✓ The distances are crucial to the initial press, both individually and collectively. The forwards must work together and make sure the center backs do not switch the point of attack.

- ✓ There are a number of 1v1 situations that develop early in this exercise. Defensively, players must be aggressive but careful not to overcommit and allow the possession team easy scores.

- ✓ In the transition phase, movement is still important for the black team. The white team will naturally look to get compact quickly so the forwards on the black team must create space and stretch the defensive line. Do not allow them to run in straight lines.

Exercise Four

Set-Up:

This tactical game is designed to help provide players with a reference point for their defensive pressure. It was designed by Pedro Mendonca in his excellent book, 'Tactical Periodisation'. The exercise takes place within an 11v11 game that has been coned off to create four 10x10 yard squares in each corner of the halfway line.

Session Details:

Both teams start in traditional positions. The team in possession provide width and depth, while the defensive team are compact. The game always starts from the goalkeeper, who passes a ball to either fullback with their feet or hands. No opposing player is allowed in the same square as the fullback when the ball is with the goalkeeper. As soon as the ball is travelling to the fullback, the opposition are allowed to press aggressively and attempt to recover the ball. If they win the ball in the same square in which the fullback received it, they score a point. If the team in possession can transfer the ball outside of the square, the game continues as a normal 11v11 game with a goal being worth three points. When the ball goes out of play, the game restarts from the goalkeeper whose team won possession. The exercise lasts 8 minutes, with a 2-minute break between exercises.

Progressions:

✓ Start the game in the middle area where teams must compete for possession and then play back to their own goalkeeper. This challenges the goalkeeper to distribute from a 'live' ball.

✓ Allow the defensive pressure to arrive sooner or later, depending on whether you want to challenge the pressing team or the team in possession.

✓ Add a 'free' player' to give the possession team an overload and make it more difficult to press. You can also counter this by awarding two points for any ball recovered by pressing.

Coaching Points:

✓ The cue for the aggressive pressure is when the ball is travelling to the fullback, not when the fullback controls the ball. Therefore, when the ball travels, the opposition travels.

✓ Remember to focus on the distances within the pressing team, especially the weak side defenders and midfielders. They must also move aggressively and have a key role to play in the shape of the team.

✓ If the team in possession are successful in playing out of the square, how do the defensive team react? Should they continue the press or recover in a defensive position? Who is making this decision and why? These are all scenarios and questions that should be understood.

Exercise Five

Set-Up:

This is an exercise from Arrigo Sacchi's 'Coaching the Italian 4-4-2' that can be used to set defensive team shape in set moments of the game, as well as transitions. It can be used as a warm-up or the intensity can be adapted to make it a fitness exercise. Eleven players are used and six cones are set out, three on each side of the pitch. If the coach wants to use more players, they can put two players in each position and alternate each team. Each cone, on both the right and left side of the pitch, is given a number between 1-3.

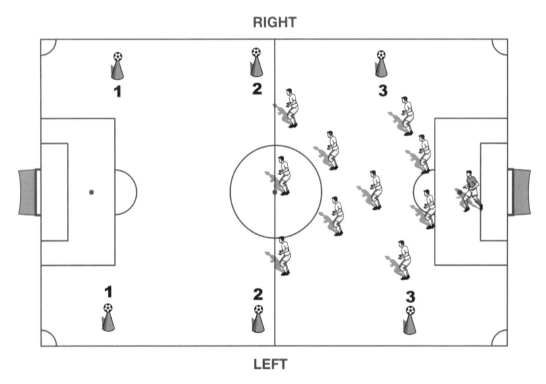

Session Details:

The coach gives the team an initial shape for a starting point. In the example on the next page, the white team are set up in a compact 4-3-3 inside their defensive half of the pitch. Coach then triggers the beginning of the exercise by shouting a side and number that the team must adapt immediately to. The following example is "RIGHT – ONE!" The team have six seconds or less to get in defensive shape. Once the team arrives at the position, they have twelve seconds to recover back to the starting position before another cone is called. This is repeated for 8 minutes.

RIGHT

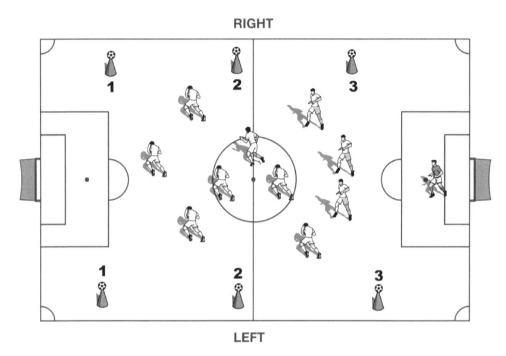

LEFT

Progressions:

- ✓ Constantly change the numbers or even use opposite sides to keep players focused and challenging them to communicate with each other. If players go the wrong way, apply a small team penalty so that they hold each other accountable.
- ✓ You can increase the physical demands by reducing the recovery run to the initial shape from 12 seconds to 8 seconds. You may have to adapt the time depending on the level of your team and stage of the season.
- ✓ Another way to increase the physical demands of the exercise is to remove the recovery aspect of it and have players constantly moving from cone to cone.
- ✓ As a coach, you may want your team fluid defensively in two systems so you can use this exercise to explain the roles and responsibilities in each one.
- ✓ Players can also be put in different positions and the shape can be adapted to suit the desired system.

Coaching Points:

- ✓ Every coach will have different systems that can be applied in this exercise, but the key principles of any system will be width and depth. How compact do you want your team, both vertically and horizontally? Use this exercise to set clear objectives in the pressing and transition phases.
- ✓ The exercise allows the coach to set different changes or tweaks to the pressing system.
- ✓ Although the physical demands may not be high for the goalkeeper, they do have a key role here both in communication and understanding distances. Do not allow the goalkeeper to stand and observe throughout, but rather remain focused and pass on information that will help players.

Exercise Six

Set-Up:

This is a three-part exercise devised by Jed Davies on compacting play, both horizontally and vertically. Team shape must constantly move in relation to the ball. All games below are 11v11 but can be adjusted to 9v9 or 7v7 to suit distances or manipulate themes. The first game is designed to compact play vertically and the field is split into four equal zones.

Session Details:

The game starts as a regular 11v11 game with one team being designated as the defensive team (black team above). In this particular game, the black team must occupy two defensive zones at all times: they must be in the same horizontal area as the ball, and the neighbouring zone closest to their goal. If they do not do this within three seconds, the opposition score a point. The flow of the game is never interrupted and the players must find a balance between intense focus on shape while still trying to play and win the 11v11 game. Therefore, play should not stop when the black team are in possession and players are also challenged to successfully transition offensively.

Progression 1:

The same rules now apply for the second game but we are now focusing on horizontal compactness. Again, the defensive team must be in the same area as the ball, along with the zone directly alongside it. The team have three seconds to get every player within the two zones or a point is awarded to the opposition.

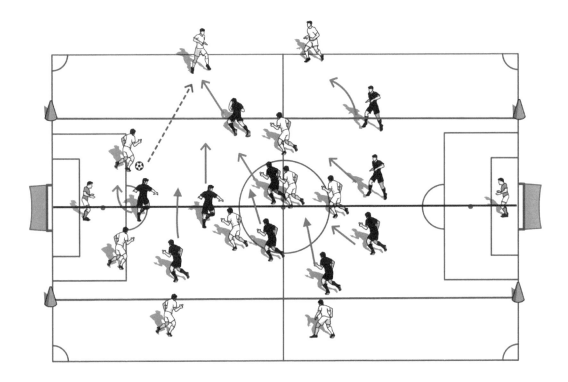

Progression 2:

The second progression combines both games with the defensive team now having to keep vertical *and* horizontal compactness at the same time throughout the game. The same scoring systems apply.

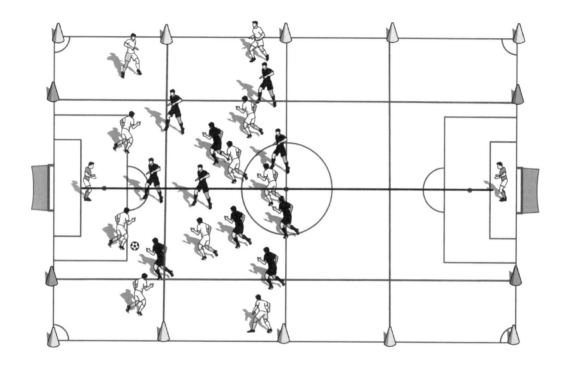

Coaching Points:

- ✓ Communication is crucial throughout the exercise. Players should not be relying on the coach or scoring system to keep their shape, and instead should be helping each other throughout the game.

- ✓ Show to the touchline by blocking off the inside. In other words, when the ball is central, all the defensive players must be in the central channels.

- ✓ Always leave the wide player free before the pass and get ready to pounce. If they man-mark initially, they are inviting the ball to be played in behind.

- ✓ When it goes into wide areas, players must get tight and be prepared to double up in support to win the ball back.

- ✓ Jed uses the phrase, "The touchline is our best defender." It narrows the angles and makes it difficult to create for attacking players.

Exercise Seven

Set-Up:

This is another one of Jed's exercises and focuses again on 'Touchline Traps' and using wide areas to draw teams into a win the ball. The exercise takes place as an 8v8 game, on a reduced field, with two wide channels.

Session Details:

Again, the game is 8v8 with no restrictions on movement or touches. If the team in possession plays the ball into a wide channel and then back out, they are awarded one point. If the defending team 'trap' them in the wide channel and win the ball, they are awarded two points. In order to make sure the game is realistic and still has a strong element of verticality to it, goals are worth three points.

Coaching Points:

✓ Distances are crucial for defenders. And balance is the key. They must stand off far enough to invite the pass, but not far enough where the wide player in possession can get back out easily.

✓ The team must adapt to the ball going into the wide zone, not just the wide player who applies initial pressure. The goal is to compress the area horizontally so the player in possession has limited options and must go back.

✓ If the team in possession successfully breaks the wide trap and plays out, the defensive team must regain shape as quick as possible and avoid penetration in the middle of the field that could result in a goal.

Exercise Eight

Set-Up:

This is a game that incentivizes players and teams to press higher up the pitch and rewards those who can do it effectively. Players are organized into two teams of nine players each, including a goalkeeper. The playing area goes from both 18-yard boxes and is split into three zones, which alters depending on the team. For example, both teams defensive zone is 1, middle zone is 2, and final third is 3.

Session Details:

The exercise begins as an 8v8 game with no restrictions in terms of movement or technical requirements. The scoring system should dictate the defensive intent and intensity of the game. If the defending team win possession in Zone 3, they are awarded three points, if they win possession in Zone 2, they are awarded two points, and one point is awarded for possession won in Zone 1. A goal is worth 5 points. Teams will play three 6-minute games with a 1-minute recovery between each one.

Progressions:

✓ Have the players organize the system of play that they want to adopt. Empower them to create a tactical game-plan that will allow them to have numbers to press and recover in the right areas.

✓ The coach can manipulate the scoring system depending on what they want to achieve. For example, if it's exclusive to high pressing and not as much emphasis on recovery shape, only award teams points for possession won in Zone 3.

✓ Add a transitional challenge to the exercise by increasing the scoring challenge to two completed passes after possession is won. This should add more focus to secure, keep or progress the ball in offensive transition.

✓ Expand the game to 11v11 and play on a full field. Now the physical requirements have increased in both pressing and recovery.

Coaching Points:

✓ Each team should attempt to apply aggressive pressure in Zone 3 as soon as the ball enters.

✓ Transitions are a critical aspect of the game. This will change depending on where they win the ball. For example, if a team wins the ball in Zone 3, they should counter and attack the goal directly, but if a team wins the ball in Zone 1, it may be a better option to keep possession and build an attack.

✓ Once the tempo begins to drop and if players begin to get tired, how does the team react in terms of their shape? For example, is it a better idea to drop into a medium block and keep the game compact? These are questions that players should be aware of.

Exercise Nine

Set-Up:

This exercise is designed to press in one half of the field, with the objectives of preventing forward passes into areas as well as stopping the switch. Play takes place inside one half of the field, with 13 players, including a goalkeeper, and two mini-goals.

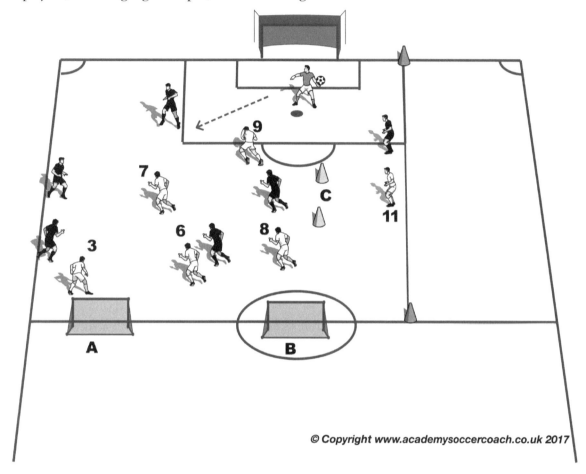

Session Details:

The example used is aimed at a 4-3-3 (black team) defending against a 4-4-2 (white team) building up in possession. The ball starts with the goalkeeper who plays a center back and then triggers the begging of the press. The objective of the black team is to play a forward pass into the mini-goals (A or B) or pass through C, which would switch the play in a game situation. If the white team win the ball, they can counter in the main goal.

Progressions:

    ✓ Add more players to the team in possession (another central midfielder or attacking player to play higher up the pitch). This would challenge the defensive shape of the white team and they would have to adjust accordingly.

Coaching Points:

    ✓ Establish the trigger to press aggressively. Depending on the numbers, it may be the first pass (even numbers) or second pass (defending team are outnumbered).

    ✓ The defensive team must force play down one side and keep it there. The body shape of pressing players should dictate this at all times.

    ✓ Because there are two goals for forward passes, the defensive team must prevent the attackers from turning or penetrating in the middle of the field.

    ✓ Watch for communication from all players and make sure that defensive shape is maintained.

Exercise Ten

Set-Up:

This exercise is designed to press opponents with a back four and prevent them from switching the play. The example we are using for the defensive team (black) is a front three and two attacking midfielders.

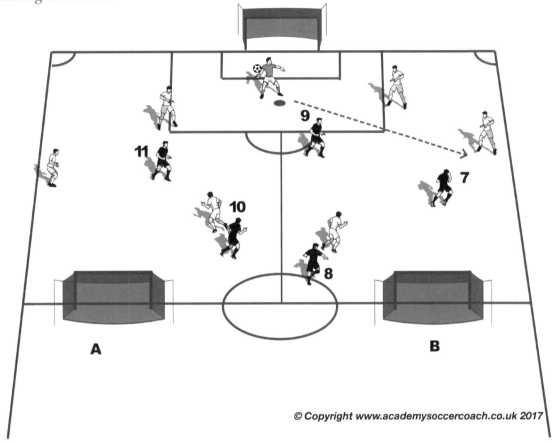

Session Details:

The ball always starts with the goalkeeper, who must play the ball to either full-back. The first pass is the trigger to begin the press for the black team. The goal of the team in possession is to score in the opposite goal in which the first pass was received. For example, if the goalkeeper plays the left back initially, the white team must try to score in Goal A. If the black team are successful in winning back possession, they can counter and score in the main goal.

Progressions:

✓ Overload the team in possession (white team) in the central midfield to create a 3v2 situation. Now the defensive team have to solve the overload centrally by either risking giving up the weak side or bringing the weak side forward in to provide cover.

✓ Create starting positions for the defensive team so that must work harder, in terms of longer distances, to apply pressure on the first pass.

Coaching Points:

✓ Encourage the black team to invite the first pass wide from the goalkeeper. Although they may enjoy higher success rate by man-marking and their direct opponents, this would not transfer to the game where the goalkeeper would opt not to give the ball to a defender under pressure.

✓ Establish the roles and responsibilities of every player from the first pass. The strong-side wide forward (#7) must apply aggressive pressure to the ball. The center forward (#9) must cut off the center backs and be in a position to challenge the goalkeeper if it goes back. The weak side forward (#11) must tuck inside to cover the space and support the center forward. That leaves the central midfielders (#8 and #10) to man-mark and prevent their opponents from turning and opening up the play.

✓ The goal of the defensive (black) team is to keep the players down one side. This should dictate the body shape of every player, who must look to stop the switch at all times.

Summary

✓ A player's positioning before the press can dictate whether they actually get an opportunity to implement it at all. Inviting the press is all about an appreciation of distances and the discipline to commit to without giving into the temptation of tight marking.

✓ By covering the space in-between players, as opposed to man-marking, the defensive team are not only inviting the ball to be played into areas where they can apply pressure, they can also send multiple players within short distances and create a numerical superiority.

✓ Preparing for opposition tendencies can prove to be a highly effective exercise to aid team performances. If you do not have a scouting system, identify the key characteristics that are prevalent with teams at your level.

✓ A traditional 4-3-3 is designed to filter possession to wide areas and press aggressively from the front line. Multiple lines of cover and the creation of potential overloads on the counter attack are strong benefits, whereas if the opposition switch the play, the system is vulnerable on the weak side.

✓ A traditional 4-4-2 allows teams to press high aggressively from the central areas, but can also be used to 'show' teams into wide channels and then double up on coverage. It is important that teams have support structures in place and are not limited to only one or two lines of pressure.

✓ Being too aggressive with the approach, not communicating with one another, reacting to the opposition's movement, allowing them to turn in central areas and consecutive forward passes, are all common ways that the high press gets exposed.

✓ Jed Davies broke down pressing triggers into four key categories:
  ○ Attacking team are not yet organized
  ○ Opponents' conditions for control are not present or are yet to be created.
  ○ Patterned traps
  ○ Pressure in relation to risk

8

Characteristics of High Pressing Coaches

Having already studied different playing models, training methodologies, position-specific profiles, as well as opposition tactical systems, we now turn our attention to some of the best proponents of pressing systems over the past ten years. In order to understand successful defensive systems, we must also look at the philosophies, beliefs, and policies of the coaches who have dominated in this area. In this chapter we will look specifically at:

- How have they built and fostered strong team spirit?
- Who inspired them on their journey as a coach?
- What specifically shaped their coaching philosophy?
- What are the key aspects of their daily training program?
- How have they achieved major buy-in from their players?
- How is their playing system set-up and are they willing to change it at certain times?

As a coach, I believe that there are two fundamental areas in which you have to work to improve your team. Firstly, your work on the training field is obviously very important. How effectively a coach can paint relevant pictures, the teaching that takes place on a regular basis, and the formation of effective training habits will always play a huge role in the success of a team. The second area, which is always slightly overlooked in my opinion, is centred around the culture that the coach creates, both with the power of their personality and the overall environment that they are responsible for. Without a culture that drives the right attitude and winning behaviours every day, the team will never live up to its potential no matter how talented they are. In addition, when it comes to implementing a pressing system, the importance of culture cannot be overlooked. You are now requiring players to push themselves at their maximum, and in many cases, perform at a level of intensity that they only visit occasionally. We must therefore look to the top coaches in the world for clues on the best way to do this with our teams and personalities. Do these coaches share common characteristic traits or operate in similar ways? That is what we will examine in this chapter.

Jurgen Klopp

"Physical problems come when you get tired in the mind, then the body follows." (Jurgen Klopp)

Although we have discussed his gegenpressing earlier in this book already, Klopp's personality and coaching philosophy is just as intriguing. Despite his playing background being widely dismissed as unspectacular, Klopp did have a 15-year professional career, with the majority of it spent at Mainz 05 in the Bundesliga, before becoming their longest serving manager from 2001 to 2008. In 2008 he joined Borussia Dortmund where he led them to back-to-back Bundesliga wins in 2011 and 2012. He enjoyed continued success with his Dortmund team during that time, including a run to the Champions League final in 2013. After leaving to take a sabbatical at the end of the 2014-15 season, he joined Liverpool in October 2015.

Any discussion of Klopp's pressing system must also address the issue of player fatigue which seems to be a topic of much contention. It seems that any time Liverpool fail to win, the argument arises on social media that his players are too tired to maintain a pressing system throughout a traditional English league campaign. 'Experts' believe that his training is not periodized, his team are overworked, and players are more susceptible to injury because of the type of aggressive system Liverpool play. I believe the basis of the criticism stems from the public perception of Klopp. Around the same time that he was introduced to the football world at Dortmund, Klopp joked that he preferred heavy metal to the orchestra type football of Arsenal. Because of this, a perceived image of a coach was born as an eccentric, extrovert with a manic touchline persona who has no regard for science and will do whatever it takes to win. In studying Klopp, however, I feel that this does not do him justice. As he disagrees and defends his methods, Klopp comes across as an extremely deep thinker of the game and does a phenomenal job in educating coaches on just what pressing is and how we need to analyse it ourselves. For example, if the critics look at pressing as a specific volume of running that players must commit themselves to in every game, regardless of score or opposition, Klopp sees that there are a number of changing variables that impact physical output and different types of games bring a different set of physical demands to a team. Below are Klopp's responses to the claims that tiredness was the reason for mid-season defeats to Southamton, Swansea, and Wolves.

"The figures are still as high in all parts as they were before, especially in distance. The games are different so there are sometimes fewer sprints to do. You can sprint, but where do you want to sprint? In this direction might make no sense. That changes in a few games. It's completely different when you play Manchester United, Manchester City or Swansea City. There's a big difference. So no, they didn't change. It's not a fitness problem until now."

"Football is about decision-making. You have to make the right decision at the right moment, and obviously we didn't do that often enough. We don't look for excuses. We don't say it's about judgment that we don't win any more, or something like this, we are 100% sure it's our responsibility. But decision making has changed."

"We don't run less, we don't rest less. In one or two games we created less and that comes back to decision-making, playing the right pass because we didn't see him, but it's still a process. It was still a process when we had a few good games and we thought that we

were flying from now on. Unfortunately, the season is too long for that. When you stop flying it's hard work to get back into this mood. Other teams will have this situation and we hope we will have already sorted it. It's not a bigger thing. It was not good enough in a few moments in the last few games and that changed the results completely."

Klopp Up Close

Although the majority of Klopp's press conferences are directed towards the news reporters and fans, he offers coaches many insightful views and opinions on the game. Klopp does not seem to aggressively push his philosophy onto people, but he has no problem discussing or defending it. He deals with criticism and praise very similarly, and shows a refreshing level of humility in front of the camera. Below are some of his quotes that fit around his philosophy and his culture at Liverpool and Dortmund.

Motivation to Coach - Like many top coaches, an unfulfilled playing career has played a part in his development and motivation to coach. "I love it because I was always a little bit frustrated about my own skills and now I work only with world-class players together, so that's pretty cool. All the things I had in my mind they have in their legs and their mind, that's pretty cool. They need only a little bit of pushing left, pushing right, giving a few informations, and then it looks pretty good to be honest."

Klopp Philosophy - "I believe in a playing philosophy that is very emotional, very fast and very strong. My teams must take it to the limit every single game. It's important to have a playing philosophy that reflects your own mentality. I've watched so many matches in my life, it's unbelievable. There are some boring games and then I sleep. It's so boring I think 'why they meet each other and make the 20, 40, 50, 60, 70, 80, 100 people watch this boring game? It's not OK. So that's what we want to see, we want to enjoy our own game."

Relationships Key - Robert Lewandowski, who played under Klopp at Borussia Dortmund, believes that the ability of the German coach to foster relationships is one of the biggest reasons why players are willing to go above and beyond for the team. "He is like a father figure, and because you have that trust in him as a player, it makes you totally open to his methods and his ideas which, in the long term, you always see are for the benefit of your game and for the team."

Ruthless Side - The smiles and the hugs can sometimes be misleading and Jurgen Klopp certainly has a ruthless side to his management style. After dismissing Mamadou Sakho from Liverpool's pre-season tour of the United States for disciplinary reasons, Klopp explained where he draws the line on commitment. "If you are full of motivation as a player, if you are full of concentration, full of readiness and passion as a player, I'm not hard, I have open arms. If you are not, of course I am hard, but only because to work with players who don't understand the professional part of this life, it's a little bit of a waste of time."

Role of the Crowd - Of course, the crowd has the ability to create an atmosphere that energizes the team, allowing them to press and play an up-tempo style. After a tense game with Sunderland, he warned the fans that tension in the stands can have a negative effect on his team. "I think we all need to learn to handle a situation like this. We're after football solution, work on it and all that stuff, that's what we try all the time and do all the time."

Teamwork Over Individuals - Klopp believes that everyone operating at maximum effort is a necessity in this game, rather than a luxury. "You can beat the best players with a team of less skilled players. That is what I love about football. It is the only game where you can have 80 per cent of the play and lose against Burnley. In no other game, in basketball or whatever, could that happen. It's impossible."

He's Human - In an era of insecurity and defensive coaches, Klopp is one of the few at the highest level who is unafraid to say that he made a mistake. During the 2016/17 season, where he is on track for his highest Liverpool league finish, Klopp has already admitted that he should not have celebrated with Sadio Mane against Arsenal, passed a mystery note to Daniel Sturridge against Southampton, or refused to give the players time off during international break.

Team Growth - Liverpool assistant coach, Pepijn Lijnders identified team spirit as a key area that Klopp is always developing with the team. "Jurgen creates a family. We always say: 30 per cent tactics, 70 per cent team building." During a February 2017 training camp in La Manga, Klopp refused his Liverpool players their own room at the five-star hotel. Instead, in an effort to find out more about each other and build team spirit, he paired them up. He also famously made the Christmas party mandatory in 2015, despite losing 3-0 to Watford, and did not allow anyone to leave before 1am. "Whatever we do together, we do as well as we can – and tonight that means we party."

Big Picture - Klopp firmly believes that high, aggressive pressing gives his team a psychological, as well as tactical, edge over the opposition and they can draw additional energy from it. "Ask a boxer: they attempt 100 punches, and the 95 which do not connect are totally exhausting. But the five which they can place on the opponent make the boxer feel world-class. This is the goal of our actions: Players should realize that the effort they are doing is worthwhile."

Running is not the Goal - Contrary to public belief, Jurgen Klopp does not have target distances for each player to hit physically in every game. In fact, progress in his system should lead to *less* physical work, as opposed to more of it. "The more dominant you can play, the less you have to invest in running."

Recovering Shape Quickly

"That's how football works - you close one hole, unfortunately you open another one. It never ends, it never ends!" - Jurgen Klopp

Part of what sets Klopp apart is his ability to accept reality that his press can be beaten and may not work on certain days. This incentivizes him to focus on how to recover quickly if the press is broken and how to re-establish a defensive shape as quickly as possible.

This is an exercise Klopp did with his Borussia Dortmund team. It takes place ten yards either side of the halfway line. The field is split into four areas across the field and each area is occupied by a defender with an attacker directly opposite. As they match up together, there are two additional attacking players on the outside sidelines. There will be a goalkeeper behind the four defenders on one side and a coach will act as a server behind the attackers on the other. The first part of the exercise involves the four defenders and the four adjacent attackers. The two wide attackers are not part of this. All players stay in their own area. The attacking players pass the ball square and each time the ball arrives at an attacker's feet, the defender directly opposite steps up to apply pressure. As the attacking player passes the ball square and the ball leaves the area, the same defender retreats to their original line. It is a simple exercise of pressure, shifting, and covering but also allows defenders to pick up cues where they will be able to see the ball arriving by the body shape of the passer. This can be hugely important in games because you can then apply pressure quicker and reduce the options of the attacker. (See below)

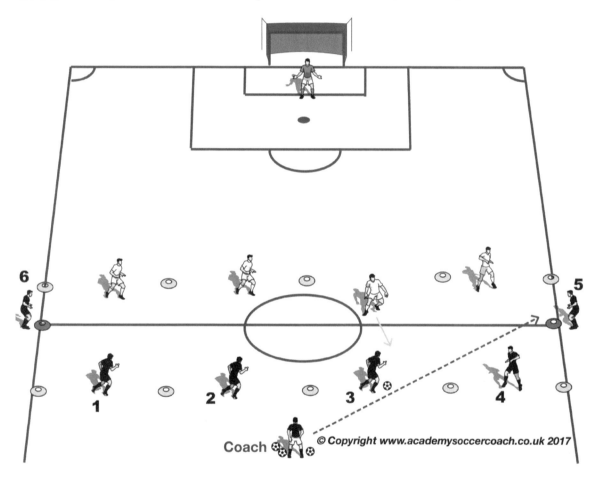

On the coach's signal, the exercise transitions into a 6v4 towards goal. The ball used in the first defensive positioning exercise is now out of the exercise and the coach triggers the ball into one of the wide players to start the attack towards goal. The first role of the defenders is to retreat towards goal but also to stay balanced. Success defensively relies so much on both individuals working together as a group. If one person switches off, especially at the highest level, it will almost certainly result in a goal. Communication is vital but when this exercise is transferred to a game in a stadium packed with 80,000 people, everyone must be on the same wavelength. The discipline to establish roles and responsibilities must be done on the practice field at full speed.

"Everyone chips in and does that in the team, from the front to the back. Even the goalkeeper has to be switched on and not so static on his line. It definitely has to work as a team. If one or two don't do it then it doesn't really work. It's quite easy to play around the press if that happens. But if everyone does it as a team and you're all tuned in to the same thing then it becomes a lot easier. It's not about individuals, it's all about team work." – Jordan Henderson

Liverpool Tactical Analysis

Match analyst, writer, coach and creator of @SidelineReview, Alistair Bain, analysed Jurgen Klopp's Liverpool when they met Tottenham Hotspur on August 27, 2016. This particular game is relevant because we can see how Klopp reacts to playing against a team that will press him with the same intensity and purpose as he does himself. Below is Bain's analysis of the Liverpool defensive shape and how they dealt with the press.

Defensive Shape

Liverpool made a decision to press in a more man oriented A-symmetrical fashion, working off of the forward motion of the ball to apply pressure to the Spurs back line & quickly take away the passing options. When pressing on the right side for example, Firminho (11) sets the first line of press by moving to split the center backs and press the player in possession aggressively. Mane (19) approaches the opponent's ball side full back and marks him tightly to avoid any easy build out from the back pattern. On the weakside Coutinho (10) moves over to pick up the opponents weak side center back, further denying any switching patterns through the opponents back line. Underneath these three Lallana (20) or Wijnaldum (5) applies pressure to the now ball side central midfielder, doing so to their inside shoulder forcing play to the sideline. In a similar vein to Tottenham, Liverpool also position Clyne (2) and Milner (7) to move forward and press the ball side winger and deny any ability for them to receive the ball and turn to face forward.

Beating The Press

To counter Tottenham's high press, especially when they found themselves fully marked on goal kicks, center back Matip (32) used Coutinho's (10) inside left channel as a target in which to play a direct forward ball. This action forced Alderweireld to come out of his zone to attack the ball, leaving the less athletic Vertonghen to deal with the pace & athleticism of Sadio Mane (19) should an attacker win the initial flick on. Fortunately for Liverpool this happened on a number of occasions, which saw Mane's (19) central movement becoming a more prominent feature. His electric pace would threaten the most competent of back lines, but his ability to move centrally in between center back & full back, latching onto play, almost looked as if he was unmarked.

Anson Dorrance

"It is critical to establish standards. Never endorse what is below standard and your praise will have meaning. Never set a standard that can be easily achieved, and your expectations will create an environment where your athletes are on edge of their game. It is time spent on this edge that improves your players. The truly great practices occur when we keep them on this edge the longest. (Training Soccer Champions, Dorrance and Nash)

In women's soccer, there is no coach quite like Anson Dorrance. Imagine the dominance of Bill Shankley, the competitive drive of Sir Alex Ferguson, the grace of Arsene Wenger, and the intensity of Pep Guardiola. If that sounds like a pretty serious combination for a coach, then we are getting close. Anson Dorrance's influence on the women's game in the past 30 years has been nothing short of sensational. Among many career highlights, he has won 21 of the 31 NCAA Women's Soccer Championships, coached a team to a .935 winning percentage, and was the first American coach to win the Women's World Cup in 1991. He may have been a trailblazer when it comes to the pressing game, but he was also ahead of the curve when it came to culture. At an early stage of his coaching journey, he went outside the sport for influence on training methods and culture, watching the UNC basketball team practice in the 1980s under legendary coach Dean Smith. Dorrance was taken back by the level of organization in the practices and the fact that Smith had a number of student-managers who were running around taking stats and recording information live during the practice. At the end of the practice, all the student managers would sprint to the scorer's table where they would submit that day's practice data into a system. By the time Dean Smith had finished addressing his team at the end of the practice, he would turn around and receive a ranking of each player's output from the session. Dorrance was fascinated by this level of accountability and decided to take the model and "soccer-ize it". He was one of the first college coaches who devised a training environment that would directly impact the performance of a team on the pitch. Even today, coaches from every sport travel far and wide to study the unique culture at UNC Women's Soccer. Every action, every game, every exercise is recorded and everything makes a difference. The 'Competitive Cauldron' signifies players climbing their way to the top of the ladder and fighting to reach their potential. Every day, there are winners and losers in his program and he uses that as a source of inspiration and motivation to his players. And make no mistake, everyone knows which category everyone is currently in.

Training Program

Tactically, the 3-4-3 pressing system has become synonymous with Dorrance's championship winning teams. However, it is worth noting that Dorrance is one of the few elite coaches in the world who has implemented a Player Development model alongside his tactical model. There are no surprises that their skill development training is just as intense and competitive as the games. Each score is weighted and every player is given a ranking. Fortunately for young and ambitious coaches, Anson Dorrance has no secrets. He openly shares his training methodology in his books, 'Training Soccer Champions' and 'The Vision of a Champion'. Below are exercises from his DVD, 'Anson Dorrance: Train Like a Champion' and is an example of a set of exercises that his players are evaluated on and are ranked in his team.

Bogies Drill – Back to pressure scoring drill where forwards play against defenders and midfielders compete against one another. Players start on both sides of the goal, and both goals and turns are recorded.

Top Gun – 1v1s to Cone –Two goals are used, one on the end-line and one on the edge of the 18-yard box. Goalkeepers are used and players play 1v1 for 2-3 minutes. Wins, losses, and ties are recorded.

Top Gun II – 1v1's From Halfway Line – Players are grouped in a matrix and take turns defending and attacking with each player playing everyone once. Defender serves the ball to the halfway line and forward then must beat them to score. Different points are awarded for a defensive stop, goal, shot wide, and shot on target.

Long Range Shooting – 1v1 game with two goals placed 36 yards apart, with halfway line in between. Players can shoot anywhere behind the halfway line. For 4 minutes, players go back and forth alternating between being shooter and a goalkeeper.

Power Heading – Two players face each other 40 yards apart. One player serves and the other heads. If the serve is good, player heads back to server. If the service is poor, partner clears the ball for distance. Distances are recorded and then averaged.

Long Service – Players serve long passes to partner for 4 minutes and must get 5 serves at each target distance in order to record a score. If they hit more or less than 5 at target distance, the score is adjusted accordingly.

Long Service/ Long Reception – Partners face each other 20 yards apart. Inside 2 minutes, they must serve lofted passes into their partner, who must be able to receive them with their chest. Points are awarded for "successful serves/traps" and team also is awarded points.

Triangle Passing – Players are organized into groups of three, based on skill level. Receiving player bends their run wide. Server plays a lofted pass into the receiver. Ball must "beat the back line" of cones. Receiver must be able to take lofted pass out of the air on the run. Points are awarded by server for successful serves.

"I'm building a fire, and every day I train, I add more fuel. At just the right moment, I light the match." – Mia Hamm (Former UNC All-American and US National Team player)

The North Carolina training model is constantly evolving and looking for ways to get better. Do not let the 'Competitive Cauldron' fool you into thinking that it is just about competing and defending. They also have a 'Possessional Platform' plan aimed at improving their circulation of the ball and getting the best attacking players into the best attacking positions. It is a combination of 3v3 and 5v2 games with transitions, as well as a 6v6+3 match with 'Final Pass Zones'. The objectives of this model are:

1. Increase the overall team ability to retain possession
2. Improve individual ability to keep possession
3. Identify and categorize individuals based on their possessional abilities
4. Drive this structure through competition

Again, everything is recorded including incomplete and complete passes in possession, incomplete and complete entry passes, entry passes received, goals and assists, winning team, and losing team. There is also a promotion and relegation segment for individuals that is used as an incentive to keep the games competitive and at a high tempo.

Meeting Anson

Interviewing Anson Dorrance was an outstanding coaching experience in itself. He agreed to sit down and talk with me during his trip to Los Angeles in January 2017 on one condition: that I hand deliver him a DVD of 2013 Champions League Final between Bayern Munich and Borussia Dortmund. He explained that he had the game recorded on his home system but had mistakenly deleted it. When I gave him the DVD, it was like I was handing him a time machine with a ticket for the game. He talked about how every coach should watch that game and how it is a personal source of inspiration and the perfect template of playing and pressing at a high intensity. He could not wait to watch it again. When he reluctantly began to describe his own system and philosophy, I quickly realized why he was so successful with it. His passion for the game and competitive drive is so evident in every single statement he makes about the game. If coaching defending is about 'selling' a system to your players, this man is on another level. He draws upon every team and experience like it never leaves his mind and his attention to detail is such that I cannot imagine there is a game or practice plan that he does not have a record of. Our conversation was part tactical insight and part motivational speech, and I walked away feeling energized about the power of passion and communication, and just how far both can take you as a coach. Below is the interview in its entirety.

In such a high-profile sport, it is very easy today for young coaches to become influenced by a certain philosophy and try to replicate it. Surely you did not have the same opportunity when you started applying a pressing system with your teams. What or who was your inspiration?

You coach to your own personality and I was a former defensive midfielder who wanted to head, tackle, and run. When I began coaching, I wanted to design a team that was very difficult to play against. As a result, every team I have coached on both the men's and women's side have pressed. The collegiate game in the US is a perfect game for pressing, because in the first half you are allowed one re-entry and in the second half you're allowed two, so it's a fantastic canvas to paint your pressing on. To press for 90 minutes under FIFA rules, you have to have extraordinary athletes and in the collegiate season where sometimes they are playing on Friday and Sunday, you are not capable of pressing if you're playing by FIFA substitution rules. Our philosophy at UNC is to let a player play for as long as possible, providing they are sprinting and pressing. And if any player feels like they cannot press anymore and stops sprinting, we take them off. So our whole system is designed around a player development platform of sprinting for 90 minutes.

When I watched Raymond Verheijen present his work, it made an impact on our program. During the pre-season we want to establish a 'zero point' in our training model. So say for example, you want to do 11v11 as a conditioning game, he recommended you play for ten minutes with two minutes off, then play for another ten minutes and three minutes off, and you keep doing this until the scrimmage (practice game) deteriorates to such an extent that it has lost its value. So your zero point is when you cannot sprint anymore. Basically, at a collegiate level, our zero point is about 3 ½ 10-minute scrimmages. So basically they do really well in the first three games and in the first part of the fourth, then about five or six minutes in they are all starting to fade – so now we have our zero point. Then every week, if you are using 11v11 as a conditioner, you add a minute on but keep the rest periods the same. The platform is adjusted so when you 'fail' at six minutes (of the 4th game) you end it. They do this with 7v7 and 4v4 and switch these weeks around. When Raymond was sharing this, it dawned on me: I am criticized for everything under the sun and one of the things I mainly get criticized for is that we substitute as much as we do. And so all the soccer snobs that I compete against, who are of course FIFA purists and pretend that they never substitute, are disingenuous when they tell recruits that they won't play at North Carolina because you're just going to get subbed a lot. Because when they play us, they do get subbed because they find it incredibly hard to play 90 minutes at our pace. Everyone believes they have ways to beat us, because, as Mike Tyson used to say, "Everyone has a plan until you get punched in the face." So yes, everyone can beat us, until they have to play us and then it's a different game. Coaches might think they have players who work hard, but they simply don't work like my kids do.

So Raymond's talking about this and it dawned on me where I thought, "Let me teach all the people in the room a lesson on substitutions." I threw my hand in the air and started quizzing him. I asked him "So what you're saying if you want to develop an elite player, and you have the opportunity in an environment like ours where we are scrimmaging and you can make substitutions, then if a player is tired, you should take them out?" And he said, "Absolutely". I then asked him how can he justify that because the game is a 90-minute game so why would you ask this player to play 90 minutes in a regular game, but sub them out when they fail in the zero-point philosophy. And Raymond told me that it's a question of what we choose – and here are your two choices as a coach: you get to choose whether you're going to play 11 players to full press for 90 minutes where the expectation of the counter attack is there as well – because you're not just sprinting when you're defending, you're also sprinting on attack. You get to choose if you want the standard of the game to be lowered, because the only way a player can survive 90 minutes of that tempo is if you lower the standard of your press or the number of people involved in the counter attack. Or you can substitute the player as soon as they can't sprint anymore and then challenge the player to extend that platform. And that's exactly what we do. For example, let's pretend that we have a starter and this person is a better player than the reserve, but there is no way the starter can press and join in on the counter attack also for the entirety of the first half, and they usually die around 20 or 30 minutes. What we do is say "Okay, I want you do play the game at full sprint and press and if you start to fade between 20 or 30 minutes, I'm taking you out. And when I take you out, I'm putting him in. Then you guys are playing to see who starts the second half. Therefore, if you don't do more than the other player in your time block, you've lost your starting position and now he's going to start the second half." So what we're doing is making playing time part of our competitive cauldron based on how fit you are.

And here's what the soccer snobs who criticize it don't understand: We have placed 87 players on the US full national team that have dominated roster sports from the 1991 World Cup and 1996 Olympics and every major tournament since. The nearest competitor from us is at around 17 players—and these are schools that out-recruit us on a regular basis. Stanford, Penn State, Virginia, UCLA and Notre Dame are all getting better players than us. So what we are doing with an inferior roster, is sending more people into an environment where they have to play 90 minutes and they are doing exceptionally well. Why? Because they are not required to step on the field and play 90 minutes, they are required to step on the field and *sprint* – and there's a big difference between those two development platforms. There's an illusion out there that coaches feel the best way to prepare a player to play at a full sprint is to play for 90 minutes if he's not fit. But in fact, the fastest way to get this player to play 90 minutes at a full sprint is to have them in competition with someone that is stealing his time, and if he's not at a full sprint, they yank him out of the game. That will drive him like it has with the Tobin Heaths, Crystal Dunns, Allie Longs, and this is the incentive to get my kids to be the fittest players on the field at an international level – because they are not training to play 90 minutes, they are training to sprint for 90 minutes. And there's a big difference.

As teams have become better equipped to deal with the press, both in terms of tactics and technique, do you think that it's become harder to play a pressing game?

I don't think it has become a lot more difficult to press, but in the game today you've got to have additional systems to bring to play, especially if the other team have overwhelmed an aspect of your press. For example, if we start out with a semi-flat back line of 3-4-3 and they have solved it, the alternative pressing system is a 4-2-3-1. Also, in the substitution patterns, our reserve unit might be more secure in the 4-2-3-1 so maybe the starters play the 3-4-3 the reserves play the 4-2-3-1, because the nice thing about the 4-2-3-1 is that you generally have more players behind the ball for most of the game. In the 3-4-3, what you rely on for the success of the press is your compaction and you are basically telling the other team that you are going to give them the space over the top, but you will be able to serve the ball easily and when you do I will train these three backs and our goalkeeper to snuff everything out. The goalkeeper plays a high line and is ready to sprint forward, and the three defenders are ready to sprint back, so you have to be better at getting behind our back line than we are at covering it.

The system can change based on personnel and the pressure can change your compaction, because if there is no pressure, you can't have compaction. So as your team loses compaction because you lack pressure, you either have to change your system or substitute the players. So let's assume your starters are all exhausted and your reserves don't have the capacity to press at the same rate, then maybe you switch into a 4-2-3-1 where it's basically a safer system and you also might have to sacrifice your offense. The critical tactical offensive principle of 4-2-3-1 is the function of the outside backs because if those two players are not your wingers, you've compromised your attack. But if you don't want to concede a goal, maybe you tell those outside backs to sit and now you're sacrificing your ability to create width in the attacking third. You do have an option of using the 3 midfielders to create width but that position is not typically designed for width. They are designed to sit in the seams between the opposition defensive and midfield line. So a very easy way to stop the 4-2-3-1 is if the outside backs are not going forward because the line of 3 are now called upon to give you your width. Then, your ability to create a superior numerical force around the ball is completely destroyed by the fact that your outside backs cannot get forward. So you're always sacrificing something as you make these decisions. One of my favourite clichés is that soccer systems are like a poor man's blanket. If his feet are cold and he moves the blanket to his feet, then now his shoulders get cold. And vice versa. So, basically when you select a system you can't cover everything. That's why it's important when you are coaching systems to understand what you get and what you lose. Then you must train your players to protect what they are losing. So basically, in a semi-flat back three we are protecting the space in behind and we are concerned about a team that plays with permanent width high. The problem with the permanent width high is that the three defenders have difficulty protecting the width. For example, if a team is attacking down one side of the field, the defenders must shift over and the function of the holding midfielder is to drop in and create a back four. But in transition, you don't have a covering player on either side of the defensive three so there is a vulnerability to every system. The coach must therefore train his players to protect the weakness in the system.

And that isn't as easy as it sounds. Every 'expert' knows how to beat our team and they will all say that we suck, and we then proceed to beat them. The way we play in this era, where other schools are getting better players, is the only way that we can survive.

Most people view pressing as a system only superiorly talented teams can implement. Would you disagree with them?

Yes! This year's team that we had at UNC was nowhere near our strongest. The ACC has a three team All-Conference team with eleven players on each one. We only had two players make the entire team of 33 and I didn't disagree with my colleagues. Yet, we are the only ACC team in the 'Final Four'. So this team proved that it's all about pressure on the ball and compaction. You don't have to have huge talent to press the ball. You just have to have a huge heart and you have got to be fit. Everyone has the potential to select to have a huge heart and everyone has the potential to select to be fit. So if you want to play for me, you need to have both, and if you are missing one or two of those things, you're not going to play. I love my players but if they want to play for me, they have to work.

Describe your practice design for pressing and defending?

We train our girls in closing (space) and biting (physical tackling). We do an awful lot of 1v1 play, and not just for offense. In my system, my players have to be able to tackle. I learned this a long time ago from Dettmar Cramer (Bayern Munich coach who won consecutive European Cups in 1975 and 1976) and his philosophy was that if you win 60% of the duels, you're going to win almost every game you play. So I train my players in duelling. I train them in the attacking 1v1 duel and in the defensive 1v1 duel. I also train them in the aerial duels. Every duel is important to train so we are constantly duelling in training and we want to make it very difficult for the other team. There is nothing complex about what we do.

If it's not a complex system then how come it's so difficult to replicate?

I've been doing this so long that explaining it is easy for me. I understand it so well and can communicate it to players in a variety of different ways, that I've got 60,000 ways to say the same thing until the player finally understands it. A lot of it however, is not down to the players' understanding of it. Typically, the player doesn't want to put in the work and a big part of the reason why a lot of kids do not play has nothing to do with understanding, it's just their lack of effort. So players have to make a choice.

How important is your culture when creating buy-in from the players?

Our culture is overwhelming because the legacy of the great players that have played at Carolina. Everyone is a believer. We have too many great players in the past for the current players not to believe everything we say. As recent as this year, Tobin Heath was US Player of the Year and she played here. Who was the Player of the Year in England? Lucy Bronze and she played here. Sarina Weigman was just appointed as head coach of the Dutch national team and she played here. So our players keep looking around and all of these great former players pop up so it's impossible for them to do anything except believe. And they all believe. What I cannot believe is how all of my critics don't understand how effective all this stuff is. If I were coaching against someone who had won 22 national championships, along with a world championship after coaching the national team, I would look at what he was doing and imitate it. No one imitates it because we have a culture of soccer snobs and when they are recruiting against me, they have their own philosophies because they all think that they coach at Barcelona. But they don't coach at Barcelona, they coach wherever they happen to be coaching. So we can all sit back and talk about possession and the beautiful game but you have to design a system within that culture to be effective. There are two elements to an elite game: direct and indirect game. You cannot play the indirect game just because you want to be a 'soccer god' in a bar. If you want to win, you must play a combination of the direct and indirect game. It's the same with Jose Mourinho when he was in his first stage at Chelsea. Soccer snobs criticized him for finding a way to win without possession. There are so many different ways to win and I've never understood why anyone would criticize any way to win. Why not look at all the different ways to win and ask yourself what you should select in order to win? In my way to win, I'm a former defensive midfielder, I hate pressure when I have the ball, so let me design a system that people will hate to play against and I've designed it. I could have selected to be a fan of Barcelona and people will pat me on the back as I'm losing game after game, but playing beautifully. I could be a hero in the bars while someone else is winning a world championship or national championship. No, I want to win and I've picked a way to do that which suits my personality.

Can a coach implement a pressing system and have a laid back demeanour on the sidelines?

It's hard. It's very hard. Diego Simeone is a good example of a coach who doesn't have the players that the top teams have, and I can't believe what he's done with those players. You have to get up. The first instinct for any player who plays is to rest and you can't let them rest. I mean, if you have great players you can sit there and look good, otherwise you can't. Part of what makes great players great is the drive, so if you don't have great players you have to drive them yourself. Every now and again I have to get up but I have a coach who works with my back-3 and he's off the bench all of the time. He's a raving lunatic. For me it's easy with the front-3 and defensive midfielders where it's "cover, balance, shift" but it's a lot more complicated in our back-3.

If they changed the NCAA college substitution rules tomorrow with limited subs and no re-entry, would you change your philosophy?

No, I cannot change. I won a World Cup pressing for 90 minutes with eleven players. When we played against Germany in the final, we knew what the German coach was going to do. His name was Gero Bisanz and he was the Director of Coaching for the whole of the Bundesliga. This guy was the 'coaches' coach' in the best soccer playing country in the world at that time. We beat them 5-2 because I knew they would play the ball around the back so we pressed for 90 minutes and destroyed them as goal after goal rained in. He was humiliated because he was getting beat by an American team with a 'no name' coach that PRESSED.

Tactical Analysis

Below is a tactical analysis on Anson Dorrance's team by Gavin MacLeod. Gavin is a Director of Coaching at AFC Lightning. He is a UEFA 'B' coach with a BS in Kinesiology & Physical Education, as well as an MS in Sport & Exercise Nutrition.

The UNC women's soccer team have been the preeminent figure in NCAA Div I women's soccer since its inception in 1982, winning 21 national championships out of the 35 that have been played. However, the Tar Heels have not won the National Championship since 2012 and have only made two college cup appearances since 2010.

While good by anyone else's standards, it is not the level of success that UNC has become accustomed to and can be attributed, in part, to the college recruiting landscape trending towards committing players at a younger age. At this stage, the top Div I women's programs are having to keep up or miss out by securing verbal commitments from players as young as 14. With 4 years until these players step foot on campus, if some of that talent stalls and doesn't develop much beyond the player they were at U15, then teams can be left without the necessary pieces to the puzzle that they had hoped to have. While that may have impacted the attacking prowess of a team like UNC, one thing that has remained a constant is their ability to apply pressure to the opposition and create moments of transition.

Attacking Shape Leading to Pressure

In their 1-3-4-3 shape, UNC derive their width from their midfield. When they can establish possession in their opponent's half through one of their wide midfielders, they will look to have all 3 front running forwards and 2 central midfielders come towards the ball-side. In doing so, they are hoping to exploit a 1v1 match-up on the opposite side of the field or create enough space for the opposite side WM to attack into.

By committing these numbers to the zone of the ball, UNC are setup to press immediately should they lose possession. This leads to them winning the ball back quickly in the opposition's half of the field, forcing them to play forward into tight spaces or long over the top.

This is where UNC's culture and coaching excels as they consistently instil in players the ability to react to 2nd balls the quickest and anticipate direct play very well by dropping or stepping in front at just the right time. This is such a well drilled part of the UNC team that they can go and press high up the pitch whilst almost daring their opponents to try and beat them in behind.

At the moment of the pass, their CMs and CBs are very adept at reading a pass into the oppositions feet, at which point they get "touch tight" and use their forward momentum to negatively affect the opposition's touch, or to step in front and win the ball to launch the counter-attack. They are similarly proficient at reading when balls will be played over the top, and use their physical advantages to get to balls in behind first. The UNC goalkeeper also plays a crucial role in this as she has to be equally as decisive when knowing which passes her defenders can't get to, and coming out to clear the danger herself.

1-3-4-3 Defensive Shape

Once a team has committed to playing out on one side of the field, UNC will structure their 1-3-4-3 to look like this: The aim is to create 3 diagonal lines of defense that allows for pressure on the ball and balance on the opposite side of the field should the opponent be able to switch it.

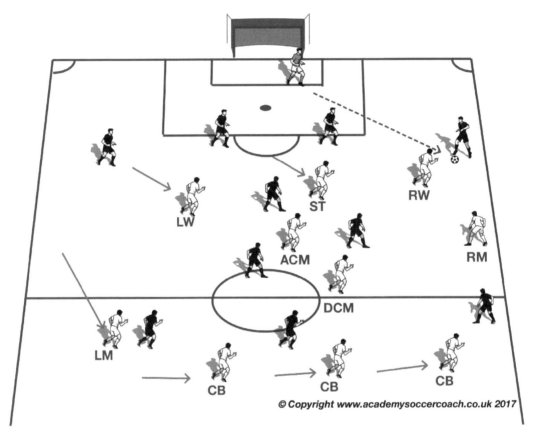

© Copyright www.academysoccercoach.co.uk 2017

Within this system, there is a lot demanded of the wide midfielders as they have to be willing to drop in to become a full-back out of possession, but then transition quickly into the attack and provide the width once possession has been regained. This is emblematic of the work ethic and levels of fitness that Anson Dorrance demands of his players, and the ability to carry out these duties are a credit to the cultural buy-in and mentality of the UNC players.

1-4-2-3-1 Defensive Shape

When things need to change, UNC have regularly turned to their 1-4-2-3-1 system, most notably in the 2012 National Championship final against Penn State. After conceding an early goal, PSU began to find some space through the midfield and in transition began to exploit space either side of the UNC back 3. When PSU finally broke through, UNC made to switch to the 1-4-2-3-1 formation which shut down the midfield possession that PSU had begun to establish and slowly shut down their ability to supply and support forward Maya Hayes.

This formation relies on a solitary forward trying to occupy the opposition's CBs, and then once play has been held to one side, UNC look to block off passing lanes into the opposition forwards, forcing passes into a congested midfield. When passes are played into the midfield, it is sometimes by UNC's design, as they quickly shut off the exits from the midfield zone.

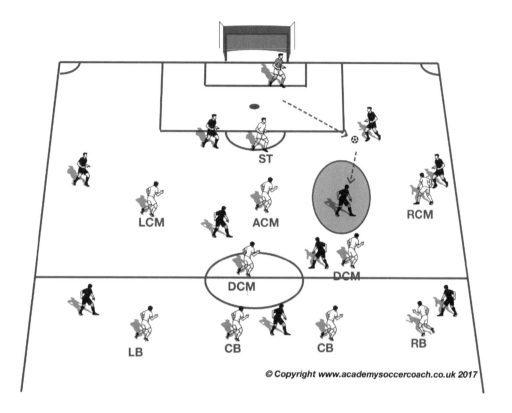

The midfielders can often take advantage of a 4v3 or 5v3 advantage and, with their ability to step out to the opposition and close off a channel to the player behind them, suffocate the zone around the ball. This becomes even more impactful when the lone forward, or other players ahead of the ball back-pressure to close down the simple outlet passes to the opponent's defenders.

Mauricio Pochettino

Growing up on a poor rural farm in Argentina, Mauricio Pochettino was introduced to long, hard days at a very early age. His family had worked the land for three generations and nothing in their family was taken for granted. His obsession with football led him to leave home at just 14 years of age to pursue a career in the game. This experience quickly built character, confidence, and leadership skills, as well as success as his 17-year playing career took him to Europe with Espanyol, Paris Saint-Germain, and Bordeaux, as well as becoming a regular in the Argentina team during the Copa America in 1999 and 2002 World Cup. After his playing career finished, coaching became a natural progression for Pochettino, taking the reins at Espanyol in January, 2009. After success in the Spanish league, he moved to the Premier League in England with Southampton and introduced a winning mentality, along with an increased work load. During pre-season he ordered triple sessions as his players would train from 10am-midday, 2pm-4pm, and 6pm-8pm. His manic work ethic is so strong that he has not only created a winning team with Tottenham Hotspur, he has re-shaped public perception of his team. Until he arrived, Spurs have been famously known as a team with a 'soft center' but Pochettino has created a team in his image. Hungry young players have quickly entered the squad and the underachievers, along with the reluctant workers, have departed at the same speed. They press, work hard, and consistently lead the Premier League in all the running charts. When Pochettino talks about his commitment to the sport, it is clear to see how he has made such an impact. "I don't have a life outside football. I spend about 12 hours per day at the training ground. Basically my life is to go from the hotel to the training ground. I am living fully dedicated to this club. In football there is not really a timetable, we just work all day long. I don't consider this work - this club is a passion."

School of Bielsa

There is no doubt that Marcelo Bielsa has played a key role in the development and philosophy of Mauricio Pochettino. As a coach, history may not judge Bielsa as one of the all-time greats in terms of winning trophies, but he will surely go down as one of the finest masterminds of the game. Obsessive behavoir does not even begin to describe the man nicknamed 'El Loco'. When he interviewed for the Vélez Sársfield job in 1997, he brought 51 tapes with him to explain how he would make the side better. This is also a man who sets a goal of two hours physical exercise per day, along with 14 hours analyzing soccer games. To look deeper into Bielsa's contribution to the beautiful game, I highly recommend reading Jed Davies' book, 'The Philosophy of Football: In the Shadows of Marcelo Bielsa'

Their paths crossed famously when Marcelo Bielsa visited Pochettino's house at 2am when he was 14 years of age, along with the head of Newell's Old Boys Academy, Jorge Griffa. After meeting Pochettino and proclaiming to Griffa, "Those are the legs of a footballer", Bielsa promptly signed the youngster. "Sometimes you need to take risks," Pochettino said. "In that moment, they trusted in a person who lived in the area. They believed, and they took a risk, and they travelled to my town. And they were very brave, because at 2 o'clock in the morning to knock on the door of a house in the middle of nowhere, you risk yourself – some dog could come and bite you – they were very brave and it's a special story."

It was working under 'El Loco' that taught him the value of analysis and preparation in building successful teams. After he bought the newspapers on Monday, Bielsa gave Pochettino the name of the forward he would be marking in the following game, and the young Argentine was to report back to his coach with a list of strengths and weaknesses. Ricardo Lunari played for Bielsa and became his assistant coach during his time at Chile. He believes that there are a number of similarities between the two. "Bielsa's and Pochettino's ideas on football are practically the same. They want to attack all over the field and base their tactics on the young players. They have different personalities, of course. Bielsa has an explosive temper and he lives matches like a mad man. Pochettino has always been a much calmer guy. But I definitely recognise Bielsa's ideas in Tottenham. Pressing was the main concept; it was the key. Even if we conceded, Bielsa would say the mistake came from not having applied the right pressure in a certain place of the pitch." Pochettino has also seen similarities between his time at Newell's Old Boys and his current Tottenham team. "If you have hunger, if you have energy, if you have potential and if you show that you have enough quality, it is perfect. And if you have some good team-mates, who give you good advice. I remember my first title with Newell's Old Boys, because I was 18 years old. If you have a good balance between younger and experienced players, it is a perfect mix to achieve big things."

Another trait that Pochettino learned from Bielsa was honesty. After being excited at the prospect of re-uniting with his 'footballing father' at Espanyol in 1998, Pochettino was asked by Bielsa to grade his form in the previous season. Pochettino attempted to remain humble and offered a modest 7 or 8, but Bielsa told him "You were s***. If you perform for me like you did last season, then you cannot play for me. And you cannot play for the Argentine national team." After driving home with tears in his eyes, Pochettino recommitted himself to the correct lifestyle required in order to meet his goals and his career took off once again. For Pochettino, it was a lesson in tough love and he is not afraid to do the same to his own players. After losing a Champion League game against Monaco, in September 2016, Pochettino slammed his players' passion and approach to the game. "The human mind is a very difficult matter to deal with. We need to accept that and work hard to try to recover it on the field. Not aggression with the opposition, but to be more aggressive with the ball, to be more hungry."

Where Pochettino and Bielsa differ drastically, however, is the relationship piece with the players. Bielsa, who famously once said that "if football were played by robots, I would win everything", never seemed to appreciate the human aspect of leadership, although one could argue that he worked in a different era. He was tough and the players both expected and readily accepted that type of management style. Pochettino however, has declared the "iron fist" as a thing of the past. He believes that a coach must play a role in helping young players find inspiration during difficult times. Technology has changed the way in which we communicate to players today, and Pochettino is well aware that coaches must adapt. Today, everything tends to make relationships colder. You have to maintain them via text messages, Whats App, Skype. It's very difficult for people nowadays to create a relationship, to look people in the eye, touch another person. Those of us that come from another generation have the responsibility to not have this new generation forget how to touch, talk to each other, relate. All of that is what football consists of. Tactics are nothing more than the relation that you have with your teammate. Based on how we relate amongst each other we will define how we act." Similar to his tactical and physical standards, it is developed every day. At Tottenham, all players must shake hands with each other every morning before training. "It is just small things but it means a lot to create a real team. You feel your team-mates, you feel your people."

What His Players Say…

Unlike Jurgen Klopp, a Pochettino pre-game or post-game interviews rarely contain sound bites for coaches on tactics, or any other side of the game. He simply does not court attention to himself or his team. His conservative and calculated approach to the media leads to minimal unwanted headlines and have helped keep his players and staff focused on the games, without the noise of distractions. When his players are interviewed, however, you get a clear picture of what is important to Pochettino and the kind of work that goes on behind the scenes at Tottenham Hostpur.

"I'm not going to lie, at the start it was horrible. Horrible. When you reach the first team as a professional, it's kind of like, 'If you want to go and do gym, do gym. If you don't, you don't have to'. But when he came in, gym was compulsory." (Kyle Walker)

"There's not been a good moment in pre-season, if I'm honest. There were double sessions, times when you were pushing yourself to the limit, but you're doing it for a reason. This is the reason that you're seeing now." (Harry Kane)

"He'd have us pressing high, keeping a high line, receiving the ball in difficult situations, keeping possession and basically having the confidence to play football rather than being afraid. The understanding in our defence was down to our training. Personally, it took my game to another level." (Nathaniel Clyne)

"It shows the great character the manager has instilled through the club, from top to bottom. A lot of credit has to go to him and his staff. We all feel very privileged to be here working under him. We've got a great team around, and it literally is a never-say-die attitude." (Danny Rose)

"Even when it was not working yet, he said: 'Do not worry, we will get there.' His speech was clear and we suddenly knew where we were going. With the quality of the workforce, and work ethic that is in training, there is no reason that we don't progress." (Hugo Lloris)

"There was always lots of running and a lot of training with Mauricio. At times it was very tough. You needed two hearts to play the Pochettino way. Goalkeeper Kelvin Davis once brought the clock out of the dressing room to remind him how long the session had been. But his methods worked. We started the 2013-14 season with just one defeat in the first 11 league games." (Jack Cork)

"For a week it was just running, twice every morning, up the hills. Then in the afternoon it was football. One week, then rest for two days, then another week. It was so hard, but it was a benefit. You feel strong, fit, faster. It is the right way." (Jordi Amat)

"Training is very enjoyable but it's physically demanding and you have to stay on top of everything, your physical fitness and mentality, but he's done a very good job and long may it continue." (Brad Friedel)

"Every day we want to improve. We beat Stoke 4-0 on Saturday but he will want everything from us as if we lost 4-0. That's his attitude and it's fantastic for us young players to be around someone who is like that, to have a manager with his attitude and work rate always working at 100 per cent and always wanting to improve. It's something we all look up to." (Eric Dier)

"He makes you suffer like a dog. And at the time, you hate him for it, but by the Sunday, you're grateful because it works." (Dani Osvaldo)

"Let's just say, if you don't work hard under the manager, you're not playing! You better make sure you give 100 per cent each day in training, which is very hard and intense. But I really enjoy it. As long as the manager sees you are willing to work hard and want to fight hard for your team-mates, then you will go far with him." (Danny Rose)

"I think the statistics show that: we outrun teams. And it's better for us because we're a young team. The more experienced players probably couldn't handle what we do, so it's lucky we haven't got too many old heads [laughs]. He's one of those managers whose door is always open. I know a lot of managers say that, but his really is. If you've got a problem in football or even outside of it, you can always go and talk to him. Those man-management skills are vital for young players like we have. It's critical to develop the squad, but we also need to develop as individuals." (Kyle Walker)

"He's world-class, not just as a manager, but as a person. The way he man-manages his players, he makes you feel good about yourself. He's had a lot of time for us and I think it shows in how well we've performed for him. He has that way about him, he's a cool guy." (Adam Lallana)

"Our practices are hard and that also helps the team to give their utmost." (Erik Lamela)

"If you're tired, he wants you to train harder so you don't get tired. You can see from the way we play that we're very fit and we play with intensity on and off the ball. Recovery is important as well but when we train, we train at 110 per cent and don't leave anything unturned. That's the way it is." (Harry Kane)

Tactical Analysis

Tim Palmer, a writer, coach, and analyst for A-League football in Australia, has provided a tactical breakdown of Pohettino's system below. Tim's website www.timpalmerfootball.com is an excellent resource for blogs and articles, as well as his Twitter account @timpalmerftbl

Tottenham Hotspur have been excellent in an unusual and unpredictable Premier League season, with a young squad featuring a much-admired British core developing a fine understanding of how Mauricio Pochettino wants his team to play. Pochettino is renowned for his emphasis on aggressive, Bielsa-like pressing. He encourages his teams to close down relentlessly when they lose the ball, introducing the concept to great success at Southampton when replacing Nigel Adkins in January 2013. The primary advantages of counterpressing are that it enables teams to disrupt the opposition's build up play, as well as creating opportunities through counter-attacks won by regaining the ball high up the pitch.

Counterpressing is not simply about pressing immediately after losing the ball, however. The four main moments of the game (possession, opposition possession and the two transition moments), while often separated in analysis, are interrelated. There are certain principles and tasks required in one in order for the team to be properly prepared for another moment. In the case of counterpressing, for example, the team must be structured and organised appropriately when they have possession so if/when the transition does occur, they are able to counterpress effectively.

Pep Guardiola refers to this with the now-famous "15 pass" rule. 'If there isn't a sequence of 15 passes first, it's impossible to carry out the transition between defence & attack. If you lose the ball, if they get it off you, then the player who takes will probably be alone & surrounded by your players, who will then get it back easily, or at the very least ensure that the rival team can't manoeuvre quickly. It's these 15 passes that prevent your rival from making any kind of co-ordinated transition."

A common rule of thumb for effective counterpressing coined by the excellent analysts at Spielverlagerug.com is "for the players to seek to occupy smaller areas of the field in a compact manner while remaining as far from each other as possible (and maintaining connection) within that small area". A team with smaller distances between players will be able to counterpress more effectively than one where they play with great width, as this increases the distance players have to cover to apply pressure when the ball is lost, and thus increases the likelihood of the opposition being able to retain the ball past this initial pressure. In this regard, it is significant that Tottenham attack with a compact structure in possession. The two wide attackers in their 4-2-3-1 / 4-3-3 system of play move into very narrow positions, with the width created by the two wing-backs who push high up the pitch.

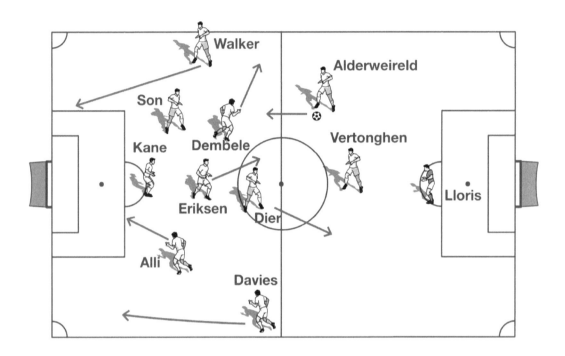

Crucially, Eric Dier, the holding midfielder, will sit in a disciplined position in front of the back four, protecting the two centre-backs and ostensibly creating a back three whereby if the opposition counter-attacks into wide areas, Jan Vertonghen, Toby Alderweireld or Dier himself can move out towards the flank to apply pressure and defend proactively. Importantly, too, Tottenham focus their passing through central areas. This means they have numbers surrounding the ball if penetrating passes to attackers between the lines are unsuccessful. These are often attempted by the aforementioned back three, with the second function midfielder, currently Moussa Dembele but previously either Dele Ali or Tom Carroll, providing support.

Interestingly, though, Tottenham don't build up play through the thirds. While they do play out from the back – with goalkeeper Hugo Lloris hugely important in this regard because of his capable distribution – they actually rarely connect attacks through the midfield zone. Rather, the centre-backs (and Dier) move the ball upfield, often quite slowly in order to give the attacking trio (formed from Eriksen, Son, Lamela, Alli, Chadli or Onomoah) time to get high up between the lines between the opposition midfield and defence. Vertonghen and Alderweireld actually play more direct than one might expect, often bypassing the midfield zone altogether by looking to hit either Kane, or release a runner in behind with a long diagonal.

Alderweireld is particularly adept at this, and to create some time and space on the ball for him, Dier will drop to the left of Vertonghen, who himself positions relatively narrow. This gives Tottenham's build up a lopsided look, evident in the diagram above.

When the ball is circulated down this left-hand side, they can draw the first pressing line of the opposition towards one side before quickly moving the ball across to the other, where Alderweireld can move forward in time and space to play a trademark diagonal forward.

The slow build-up when Tottenham have possession in deep positions is important because it gives the players ahead of the back three time to get into a compact, connected shape. Spurs are particularly good at winning second balls because they always push attackers close in support of Kane so that he is not isolated when trying to win aerial duels from long diagonals.

These specific structures and principles give Tottenham the platform to then be able to counterpress when they lose the ball. In fact, their structure for counterpressing allows Tottenham's players to attempt risky passes into the final third, because they have the ability to win it back quickly.

It may seem counteractive and defensive to prepare for defensive transition when you have possession. However, it ensures that the team maintains stable with and without the ball, and are in a position where they can win the ball from an opposition that is shifting into offensive organization – meaning, they are spreading out and thus are more vulnerable to a quick counter-attack.

This is undoubtedly a difficult concept to grasp and it is unsurprising that it has taken Pochettino more than a season to fully implement his ideas and way of working at Tottenham. However, the players now demonstrate a clear understanding of their roles and responsibilities, and are one of the league's most organized teams with and without the ball.

Brendan Rodgers

Born on the Antrim coast of Northern Ireland, Rodgers left to pursue a professional career in England when he was 18 years old. After captaining the youth team at Reading, a genetic knee condition ended his professional dreams and forced him to retire at age 20. It was then that Rodgers moved his attention towards the coaching side of the game. He began his badges with Reading and soon became Academy Director of the club. Coach education also became a priority as he made frequent trips to Spain to study both the language and culture of football. It was shortly after that he was head hunted by Jose Mourinho at Chelsea in 2004 to manage their youth team. Rodgers made an immediate impact on Mourinho and was quickly promoted to the reserve team, where he worked closely with the Portuguese coach. Every stop for Rodgers has been a learning opportunity that he has benefitted from. He also studied neuro-linguistic programming for five years.

In his early years as a manager at Reading and Watford, Rodgers favoured a slightly traditional English 4-4-2 system. It was when he joined Swansea where he succeeded Roberto Martinez, that he could implement his continental philosophy.

According to 'Outside Of The Boot', Rodger's system at Swansea revolved around three things:

- Possession (attacking with the ball and then resting with the ball)
- Moving the ball from side-to-side to open up spaces
- Defending in zones rather than a fixed formation

In 2012, Liverpool became the next stop for Rodgers. His impact was immediate. At their best, Rodger's Liverpool were high pressing machine and the "five second rules" was there for everyone to see. With Luis Suarez in frightening form, Liverpool became equally as devastating on the counter-attack, as they were in the press and came within touching distance of winning their first Premier League title in 2014. Below is a decision-making and principles chart of the game model that Rodgers used during his time at Liverpool.

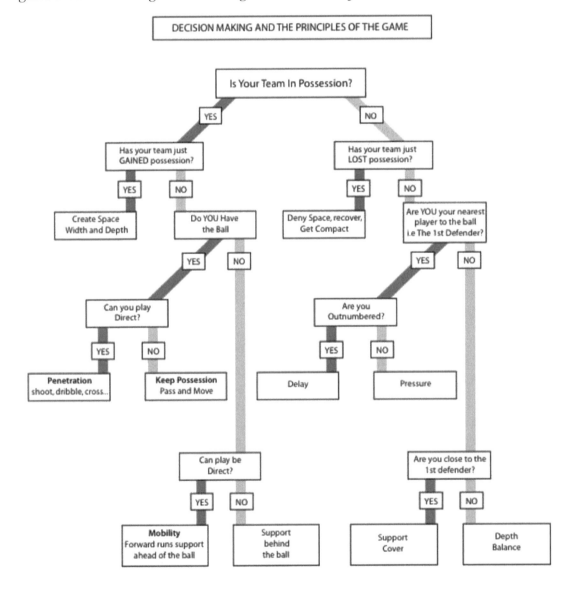

After leaving Anfield, Rodgers was announced as the manager of Scottish giants, Glasgow Celtic, in July 2016. Although the club has a rich history of domestic and European success, the financial landscape of Scotland is significantly different from that of their English neighbours, as well as most of Europe. These lack of resources have made Rodger's success in his short time at Celtic even more impressive. He has recruited well and built a game model that caused Manchester City and Barcelona many problems in the Champions League. Rodgers has taken his pressing template to Celtic where he has received major buy-in. Forward Leigh Griffiths is one of many players who has experienced benefits under Rodgers. "My game is all about pressing and getting in behind defences. He has spoken to me a couple of times and said if I get that pressing correct the people behind me will be winning the ball and I should get a lot more opportunities than I got last season."

Coaching Principles

Even for a football purist, Rodgers' philosophy is closer to John Wooden than it is to Johan Cruyff. In Michael Calvin's book, 'Living on the Volcano', Rodgers explains how he works with the professional players at Liverpool in the exact same way. "I don't see myself as a coach, or a manager. I see myself as a welfare officer. I look after the needs of the player, and the group. So I understand that that is technically, tactically, physically, mentally, but also lifestyle, socially. I work with these kids like they are my own. I give them advice like I was giving advice to my own son."

When he explains his CORE principles of Commitment, Ownership, Responsibilities and Excellence to young players, he always draws the crown on a head to represent the fact that each player is the king of their own destiny. He opts for commitment rather than motivation because he believes that motivation is fleeting as it goes by feelings. "I always say, 'It's your responsibility … the crown is on your head.' You are the king of your own destiny. Wherever you go is down to you. I enjoy being around people and I enjoy making people feel good. It's how you frame situations and negatives. I say to the players, 'If you want a problem, there is one just round the corner.' The world is full of them. Try to find a solution and be the best you can be."

Rodgers' Playing and Development Quotes

Every Brendan Rodgers interview or press conference is a learning opportunity for a coach. He is passionate about his philosophy and seems to love discussing the opportunities and threats that are presented to his team every week. Player development is also a topic that Rodgers seems to enjoy discussing, especially with the genuine interest he takes in the young players coming through. Below are some exerts from his press conferences that relate to his philosophy, playing model, and player development.

"When going forward, the best way to move the ball up the field is to create angles of diagonal pass. If you have two banks of four across defence and midfield there are no diagonal passes on. The system needs to be more fluid."

"The only time we rest is when we have the ball. When we haven't got the ball is the moment for intense pressure to get the ball back. But you can't go for 90 minutes, so in order to recuperate and conserve energy, we'll do that sometimes by building our way through the game."

"You cannot go (press) on your own. You work on zonal pressure, so that when it is in your zone, you have the capacity to press. That ability to press immediately, within five or six seconds to get the ball, is important. But you also have to understand when you can't and what the triggers are then to go for it again because you can't run about like a madman."

"At the moment every single player is fit. The training is tapered in order to maximise what they bring into a game. My physiologist Glenn does a terrific job. And there is a relationship between medicine and sports science, and the football philosophy that we have. So each day the training pitch size is all geared towards the next game. And it means the players are at the right level of intense physical loading going into every game."

"As you evolve as a manager and a coach you understand and recognize that at times there are different ways to win a game of football. Our notion in the game is always to dominate the ball. But I've been in football a long time and my emphasis has always been possession but dangerous possession. That is important to us. Our conditions of a game won't change but hopefully because of the different types of players, and different strikers in particular, it gives us that unpredictability which is important."

"At any level of work it's about achieving progress and improvement. The nature of the methodology here and how I develop players, it's about the individual for me. The needs of the individual and that goes into the collective. What happens through our work is that players and individuals improve, and when you improve as a collective then you get the gains from that."

"The point is, yes, they all want to play for Celtic. But, before you can play for Celtic, you have to be able to train with Celtic. If you're never fit enough to train, how are you going to play? So, it's important to create an elite environment. Some will fall by the wayside because it's too much. If you want to be lean, fast and strong, it's a serious business."

"That's what you need to do to be a top player. Body fat, body mass, looking after yourself, being a professional. It doesn't start when you arrive at the training ground, it starts with your first waking moment. Then when you drive out, it doesn't end. It's a lifestyle. It's right the way through. The guys that will play on until they're 35 are the guys that have been looking after their body. If you have a brain to add to your brawn, then you'll have a chance. To be an elite sportsperson at the top isn't easy. If you want to operate at the level of Champions League, be a world class player or the very best player you can be, you have to develop technically, tactically, socially, and in terms of your lifestyle."

"The job for me is continual. I live and breathe for football. I study it, I look to be better, for how we can continue moving forward. And I'm ambitious. I want the club to achieve, I want the players to achieve. I will be at the planning until I go to bed."

"We're at our best when our game is aggressive. So for us it was about trying to find the solution to get back that intensity and tempo to our game, which is critical in terms of how we work. That's key, that real aggressive pressure at the top end of the field. The players are starting to adapt and performances will get better and better."

"Nobody in the team is asked to do any more or any less than anyone else. It's the collective that allows us to work that way. And every player gives their maximum. If you're struggling for whatever reason, you come out and another profile comes in to maintain it."

Tactical Analysis

Match analyst, writer, coach and creator of @SidelineReview, Alistair Bain, again gives us a point of reference into the makeup of a Brendan Rodgers team. This analysis below is designed around a typical opponent in the Scottish Premier League and explains what Rodgers' team is attempting to do, both in and out of possession.

Opposition Structure

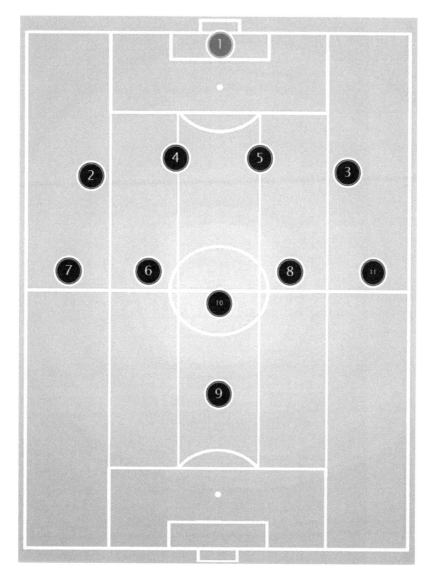

Should the Celtic goalkeeper have the ball at his feet and is about to initiate the start of up play, it's typical for the opposing side to drop back into a 4-4-1-1 shape, with both defensive and midfield lines of four retreating into their own half. The opposition striker and attacking midfielder plug gaps centrally and are primed to press forward should a Celtic midfielder dribble into, or look to build through, their central zone. The overall strategy is to dominate defensively through territorial superiority and refrain from leaving their shape to win back the ball. In reducing the size of attacking space in which Celtic can access in the middle and latter thirds of the field, they give themselves an increased chance of picking up any threatening movements between the lines, but also with their starting positions being closer to the ball when the press is activated they can implement greater numbers to press with smaller structural impact. Here are a number of factors the opposition has to constantly wrestle:

1. Maintaining the vertical space between the defensive and midfield line
2. Maintaining the horizontal distances between the midfield line, while still compensating pressure, cover and balance relative to the ball and space in front of them
3. Maintaining the horizontal distances between the back four
4. Maintaining central superiority in the defensive line, 2v1 mainly, 3v2 if midfielder joins forward
5. Maintaining the distance between the last central defender and the goalkeeper to prevent through balls
6. Maintaining their overall team shape to prevent becoming too narrow and offering Rangers an opportunity to penetrate on the outside, or too stretched and opening passing or dribbling lanes

However we regard remaining compact defensively as a strategy, the complexities of maintaining these elements for ninety minutes is a mammoth task, one that is made significantly more difficult given Celtic's heightened level of player quality.

Possession Based Analysis:

Building Shape

Building from the goalkeeper has become a signature part of Rodgers' game model and it has once again been utilized during his time with Celtic. Fundamentally the build-up pattern is designed in such a way that it primarily entices an opponent to move up the field collectively to press the ball, therefore exposing space in their own half that the Celtic forwards can exploit with their pace. Should the entire opposition team fail to move as a cohesive unit, the build pattern causes fractures in the vertical spaces between the opposing units, such as a forward breaking free from the low or medium block and therefore becoming easier to pick off through possession. The final area it exposes is the horizontal spaces between a single line of players or the diagonal distances between a striker and a winger, for example, as play shifts sideways. In essence the strategy employed in the building phase is one that allows Celtic to orchestrate a structured forward movement of the ball, increasing their chances of maintaining forward positioning and placing their attackers where they want as opposed to having to chase after a long ball. Similarly, the build forces the opponent to move away from the spaces they want to defend and unbalances their shape in doing so.

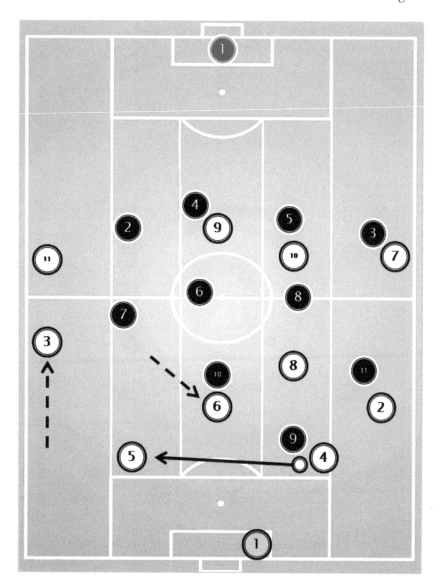

Celtic's starting formation is in a classic 4-2-3-1 shape; however, it is typically only the center backs and defensive midfielder who take part in the initial pass out from the goalkeeper. The full backs and second defensive midfielder layer themselves in front of the line of the ball, positioning themselves in spaces that work to Celtic's strategy or to pull an opponent from their preferred defensive positioning. One particular pattern of play that is often deployed sees the ball move out to the left center back, who is positioned at the edge of the box, then a pass is played across to right center back who is now turned and facing forward. As this transfer occurs the left back moves forward into a more traditional wide left position in the midfield line, essentially opening up the space in which the left center back can move into if he requires more space. A central defensive midfielder then drops into a deeper central position splitting the back two, and based on the pressure applied, the right back pulls into a wide position, however is significantly deeper than the left back. The opponent is now drawn over to the Celtic's right hand side, as there now appears to be an overload of players around the ball.

Asymmetrical Shape and Stretching Opponent

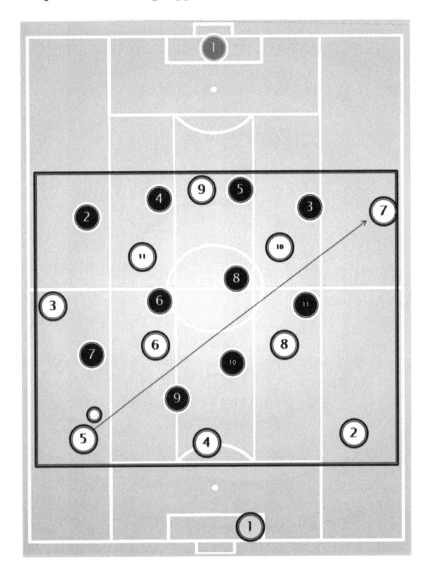

What I find to be most interesting about Rodgers' game model is the asymmetrical team shape, but also how this lends itself to stretching the opponent out over a larger area. Typically, we see a team shape expand centrally as a means of stretching the opponent's back line higher up the field vertically, thus increasing the spaces between the opposition lines of play. Rodgers' game model looks not only to achieve vertical space between the opposition, but by placing the right winger on the highest line at the widest point it also creates horizontal spaces between the opponent's defending units. Let's look at an earlier picture when Celtic built through the left center back, a position that is at the farthest point from the high right winger. This questions the opposition's ability to defend zonally on the ball side, especially if they wish to remain in their own half and stay compact. Alternatively, should the opponent choose to use a man marking system on those on the wings, this will then create central gaps between the opposition lines of defense that Celtic's player positioning allows them to expose.

Out of Possession Analysis:

Counter Pressure

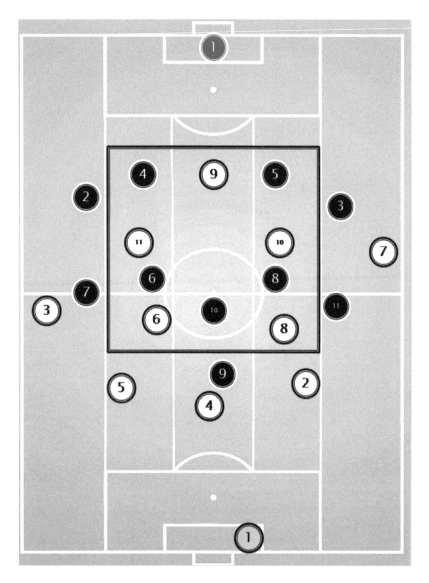

While Rodgers' Celtic side are an extremely well-functioning attacking unit, they have managed to lend some of their attacking athletic prowess to enable them to win the ball back efficiently should a turn over occur. Counter Pressure in its purest form is defending to prevent the opponent from counter attacking after a turnover has occurred; this form of counter defending has become most identifiable through coaches such as Jurgen Klopp and Pep Guardiola. Rodgers has employed his own form of counter pressure within the Celtic game model, which focuses on denying the opponent any central stability. Typically, during periods of transition, Celtic's opponent relies on their central defenders and midfielders to act as pivot points, a role which is deployed to switch play to the weak side or play a forward pass in behind Celtic's high back line. With Celtic's possession structure designed to feature 2 central midfielders, 2 central attacking midfielders and 1 central striker, in essence they have created a 5 v 4 against the opponent's shape, or at worst a 5v5 should the opposition No.10 move deeper to play. While numerically this shows us quantitative superiority or a numerical match up, positionally Celtic have the upper hand as they can press both sides of the ball in midfield and can apply pressure on the side and in front of the opposing center backs. Latching onto the ball from a number of directions reduces the natural options their opponent has to rebuild play and forces them to play a longer pass that is more reactionary and less thought out.

Forward Pressing Shape

Celtic's defensive structure from re-starts or when play is dropped back to the opposition goalkeeper sees them move into a more conventional system shape. Against typical 4-4-1-1 systems that they face in the SPFL they begin in a regular 4-2-3-1 defensive shape before advancing forward to defend, however quite often as there is no natural opposition pivot dropping between their midfield and attacking lines to allow the No.10 to move forward next to the No.9. This, therefore, alters the structure slightly to appear more like a conventional 4-4-2 when pressing. The nuances that are then inserted come from trigger points in the field, which are specifically designed to lure the opponent into building through pre-set areas of the field which then signal the start of a collective press. In the previous illustration, you'll see the Celtic No.10 positions himself away from the center back who receives the ball, as does the winger who moves inside freeing up his opposition full back. The No.10's positioning is strategically designed to prevent a forward pass into the midfielder behind him and takes the center back's attention over to the ball side full back who is essentially standing open. The instant this pass is played out to the full back Celtic's right winger presses the ball in a diagonal fashion, preventing a pass inside and giving his opponent the opportunity to pass back or pass down the line. The No.10 instantly moves up and marks the opposition center back, essentially to intercept the ball should it be dropped back into him. With the opposition full back's only real option now to play forward, it allows Celtic's defensive shape to remain compact on the ball side and only have to defend one open player, the opposition winger, or should the ball be played long and over their back four the open player now becomes a central striker who peels out into the wide area. The goal of this type of defending does two things, it reduces the space in which the opponent has to play, but it also denies them the ability to gain a possession based rhythm by moving the ball across the field horizontally.

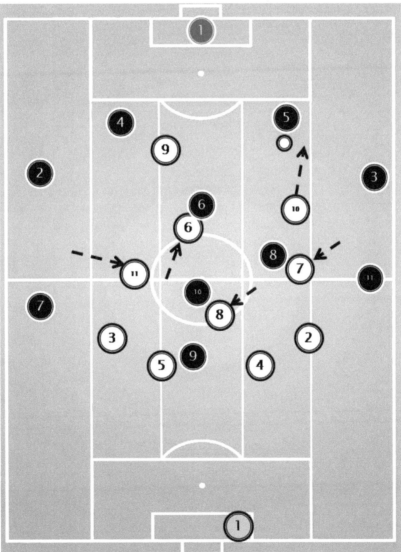

During instances where Celtic do face a midfield that allows for a natural pivot player, their defensive shape alters again in a diamond 4-4-2 of sorts. The No.10's pressing angle changes from before in that he now moves forward and actively presses the center back, this time not looking to specifically win the ball in the 1st action but to encourage the center back to in fact play a pass into his deep lying midfielder. This player is then met with Celtic's most aggressive and physically dominant midfielder, club captain Scott Brown, whose pressure on the deep lying opponent is such that he is going to win back possession. This action is met with the Celtic wingers collecting inside to form a central overload with the remaining defensive midfielder, creating a 4v3 in Celtic's favor. If a turnover does not occur during the pressing of the opposition deep lying player and play works its way out to an unmarked fullback, this would then allow Celtic to engage the same press as illustrated in the first example. They use the ball side positioning of their winger to press the full back in question, and then move across to fill the space accordingly.

9
Getting the Details Right

"Tactics will always be a part of the manager's job, but before you get to that, there's the attitude of the player and his concentration, his motivation, his desire to win. This is more a job for a human being than a coach." – Andre Villas Boas

Whether coaches today like it or not, how you communicate has now become much more important than what you communicate. Twenty-five years ago, the majority of coaching was done on the training pitch, where players were invariably told what to do, how to do it, and then expected to carry it out on command. The great Brian Clough summed up how the player-coach relationship typically worked, "We talk about it for 20 minutes and then we decide I was right." The command style was widely accepted by every player and life went on. The game today, however, has changed drastically in this area, and because we want our coaching to evolve with it, we need to ask the right questions of ourselves and our way of working. Pressing in particular requires players to commit themselves to the tactical plan, their teammates, and to the coach. It is therefore our job as coaches to find the best ways to do this.

Another reality of the modern game is that success now requires more than simply working hard. It is about constantly encountering problems and finding solutions, as quickly as possible. That applies to both sides of the ball, and now the requirements for a defensive system are higher than they have ever been before. In this last chapter, we will now look at how we can take a multi-disciplinary approach to our coaching by addressing some areas where the game has changed and affects the pressing game.

Recruitment

It seems that we have also arrived in an era where teams with less resources can outperform teams who have the luxury of more. In 2016 we saw Leicester City take the Premier League and teams like Northern Ireland, Wales, Iceland, and Portugal exceeding all expectations at the European Championship. How do so many teams prove the doubters wrong when the financial gap today is so big? Was it just really the year of the underdog? I believe that the answer lies closer to recruitment than it does towards fairy tales. The Chicago Cubs ended their 108-year World Series championship drought in November 2016 and provides an interesting lesson on how success today is achieved. Theo Epstein, president of baseball operations for the Cubs, is the highest paid non-athlete in professional sport, after signing a $50 million contract. He has designed algorithmic tests, data analytics, and programs for coaches to deal with stress management. One of his priorities in recruitment, however, is to make sure they get the right 'person' rather than the right 'player'. "In the draft room [where the team decides which players to sign], we will always spend more than half the time talking about the person rather than the player," Epstein reveals. "We ask our scouts to provide three detailed examples of how these young players faced adversity on the field and responded to it, and three examples of how they faced adversity off the field." With so much scientific and numerical data available to improve his players, Epstein wants players who have a desire to learn and develop. That level of humility is harder to find in today's sports world, particularly with players being rewarded earlier in their careers for essentially doing less than previous generations.

Again, when it comes to pressing, character matters for so many reasons. You are asking players to continually work hard for one another, sometimes without getting credit, and many times so that someone else in the team can profit from their work. In transitional pressing, you are asking them to put personal disappointment aside immediately in order to provide another opportunity for your team or to prevent the counter attack. Pressing is the ultimate character test when it comes to soccer, therefore, it is increasingly difficult to implement it with a team or a group of players who do not share the right character traits that are required. Diego Simeone is a big believer in that character correlates to a successful player at Atletico Madrid. "You are the same in life as you are at work. If you're noble, you're noble. If you're a hard worker, you're a hard worker. If you're a traitor, you're a traitor. If you don't pull your weight, you don't pull your weight. If you're selfish, you're selfish. The relationship with football is parallel."

Communication

Over a period of time, a team naturally takes on the personality of their coach. This impact typically takes place in two different areas: on the field and off the field. In October 2016, The Wall Street Journal did a report on the communication of Pep Guardiola in the Manchester City versus Tottenham Hotspur game. Again, it's a great example of two teams pressing each other and game models being tested in and out of possession. According to the Wall Street Journal analysis, Guardiola spent 52 minutes and 35 seconds 'stalking' the touchline. During this time, he directly addressed 9 of his 10 outfield players and made 25 interventions. Midfield playmaker, David Silva, was summoned on three occasions for one-to-one chats. In Chapter 8 of this book, Anson Dorrance addressed the fact that his players needed constant instructions and energy from the bench to help aid performance. Klopp never sits down, Simeone kicks every ball with his team, and Jorge Sampaoli is continually animated on the Sevilla bench. So, if this applies at the highest level, surely coaches at youth and amateur level should be following suit. Of course, there must be a balancing act on the sideline. If a coach is detached from the action it can create feelings of abandonment from the players. Alternatively, if a coach is overloading players with information, it can become hand-holding, or even worse, cause the players to tune him or her out.

Off the field, the pressure and expectations on the coach has also shifted dramatically in recent years. The last two coaches to win the Premier League with their clubs, Jose Mourinho and Claudio Ranieri, were both fired within seven months of lifting the trophy. Results obviously played a major role in both dismissals, but we cannot downplay the fact that both Chelsea and

Leicester City had a group of players who no longer believed in the coach. It is a problem that is evident at all levels of the game. So many teams today are filled with tension that is so thick it has become debilitating.

A huge part of coaching today involves finding the answer to these questions: What motivates our players? What do they think? How do they learn? What do they expect? What are you going to do to attract them, keep them, and create an environment in which they will excel?

Plenty of coaches today complain that today's young players are different. In the book, 'Managing the Millennials', Chip Espinoza and Mick Ukleja argue that the core of the millennial phenomenon is that today's generation of young people do not have the same need or know-how to build relationships with their managers or authority figures. Previous generations, like the ones most coaches grew up in, had to take initiative. That is not to say that millennials do not want to connect as they desperately want mentors and career advocates.

Espinoza and Ukleja write that today's generation share the following characteristics:

- ✓ Refuse to accept status quo.
- ✓ Trust leaders with raw authenticity.
- ✓ Expect their environment to be challenging, creative, and dynamic.
- ✓ Want coaches to provide direction and then get out of the way.
- ✓ Are the first generation of players who can access information without an authority figure.
- ✓ Use technology to do less work, whereas the coach's generation use technology to do more work.

The book also challenges leaders today to possess the following strengths:

1. Self-Efficacy – They must believe that they can do something about their situation. Problems are there to be solved and improvements can always be made.

2. Confidence – A modern coach must allow players to question and challenge them without getting defensive. If a player asks "Why are we doing this?" a coach should be able to provide an intelligent answer.

3. Power – A coach must not rely on power statements like 'Because I am the coach." If you spend more time proving yourself than you do expressing yourself, you are relying too heavily on positional power.

4. Energy – Coaches today should feel energized by working with today's players.

5. Success – Challenged managers consider millennials to be an impediment to their own personal success.

Evaluating Your Press

In Chapter 8, we addressed the criticism Jurgen Klopp's pressing system received following a string of Liverpool defeats. If we are going to commit to an extensive planning process of a pressing system, then coaches must identify how we are going to measure it effectively and accurately. Below are three areas that we should **not** use as a measuring tool for our pressing system:

Results - Even if fans or parents judge the success of your tactics by the result of the game, you must not go down the same road. No one preaches process and development like the modern-day coach, and we must realize that pressing cannot be an 'all-or-nothing' solution to every attacking problem. Your team's press might be stifling the opposition to such a level that they decide to change their system at half-time and become more direct. That change may result in an extra number up front and all of a sudden, the dynamics of a game has changed to suit the opposition, despite the success of your pressing. The reality is that an effective press can be successful in limiting an excellent team without actually beating them. If a team has an abundance of talent and a bench that allows them to change personnel and/or their attacking system, there is still a lot of work to be done.

Distances – Although running and sprints with GPS systems are a good metric to see the work rate and intensity of a team, they do not give an entirely accurate picture regarding the success of a pressing system. Pressing is reliant on the team moving in unison and therefore the direction and timing of a player's movement is a lot more important than the volume in which they do. For example, below is an example of a wide forward (number 11) on the white team in a 4-3-3, sprint forward in an attempt to apply pressure on the opposing team's center back. Although the speed and intensity of the press was excellent, the lack of positional understanding allowed the center back to play a pass into the right back, which now not only breaks the press, but it creates a 2v1 overload in a wide area. You cannot fault the work rate of the #11 as they made an initial press (A) and then attempted to recover defensively (B), but the reality is that their lack of tactical awareness and discipline has compromised their team's defensive shape. This example could happen anywhere on the field, and against top opposition, it can be the difference in a game.

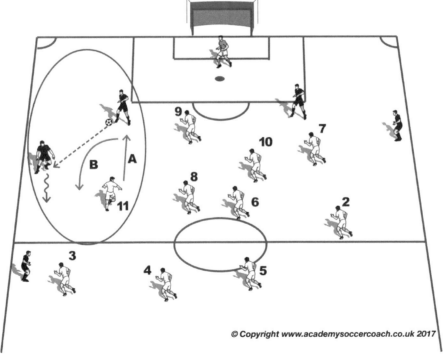

Conceded Space– A uniform pressing template will never provide an accurate picture to judge your press because different teams will always have different objectives for their defensive system. For example, the objective of one team may be to deny progression of the ball into a midfield area, whereas another team may want the ball to go there and then use it as an opportunity to force turnovers.

A common difference in pressing systems is the objective of wide forwards once they apply initial pressure to an opposing full-back like the situation in the picture below. Some coaches will want to show that player inside, towards the central midfield area, where the defending team have a numerical advantage and will have an opportunity to win the ball. Other coaches, however, may feel that by 'showing' the full-back into a central area, they will create an overload that will expose their central midfielders and back four. Because of this, the coach may instead want to 'show' the full-back outside and then create a 1v1 directly or a 2v2 with the other full-back and wide midfielder. Neither situation is right or wrong, and depends on the philosophy of the coach and whether it is effective or not.

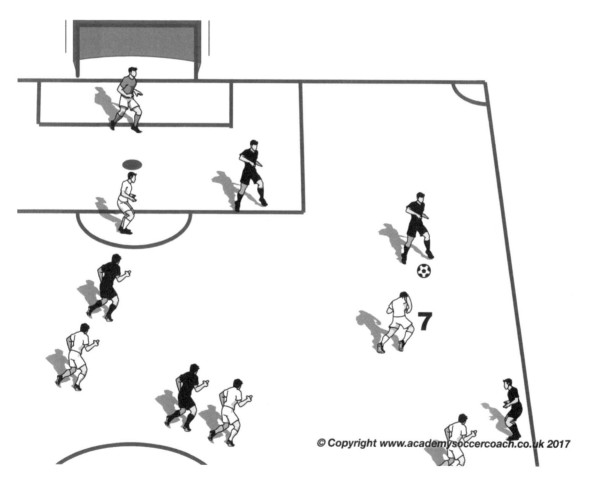

Measuring It

So, if those are not the most effective ways to measure a pressing system, what are the best ways to do it? In essence, we are looking for ways to communicate to our players where progress is being made and where we are vulnerable. If we can accurately evaluate, then we have an opportunity to sustain it and improve it further.

Defensive pressing has been measured by tactical analysts including pass completion percentages. Colin Trainor developed a PPDA model where the success of pressing was calculated by the opponent passes allowed per defensive action, in their own 3/5 of the pitch. By defensive actions he meant tackles, interceptions, challenges (failed tackles) and fouls.

PPDA = Number of Passes made by Attacking Team/ Number of Defensive Actions

Johannes Harkins at OPTA Sports then took this one step further towards a more holistic approach to measuring a pressing system. She believed that one single measurement did not give an accurate picture of pressing. For example, Paris St. Germain, who did not have a reputation for a high pressing team, yet were high on the European teams who excelled in pressing. Upon closer inspection, she found that PSG were a team who dominated possession deep in the opponent's half of the field, and because of this system, had more opportunities to perform defensive actions higher up the pitch. Her work is focused more on comparing different aspects of defensive systems and takes four metrics into consideration:

- **PPDA**: Opponent passes allowed per defensive action, in the opponent's defensive 3/5ths of the pitch.
- **Opponent Pass Completion:** Overall percentage of opponent pass completed.
- **On-ball Action Width**: Distance of team non-defensive touches from the middle of the pitch.
- **Directness**: Opponent pass distance in the x-coordinate (endline to endline) as a percentage of total pass length. Measure the degree to which passes are progressing up field.

Coaches Without an Analysis Department

How useful is the above information to a coach who does not have access to the expensive analysis equipment or is not fortunate enough to have the time or resources to analyze a series of games? I believe it is very helpful because it challenges coaches to look deeper at their own unique system and question ways to measure and improve it.

Judah Davies, an Opposition Scout for Huddersfield Town FC and Tactical Analyst for Spielverlangerung.com believes you can combine subjective and objective analysis.

Subjectively: A coach could evaluate their pressing system based on the areas that they force the opponents to play in (do we force them wide, deep etc.), how often the opponents can progress into dangerous areas and create chances, and how often they force the desired consequences: whether that's forcing opponents to play long balls or winning the ball back in the opponents' half.

Objectively: This could be drawn from those subjective measures: for example, a quick action by action notational analysis every time you regain the ball in the opponents' half, force a long ball or so. If the coach feels unable to do this during the game, they could ask someone who would be there regardless to do it, such as a substitute or a volunteer.

European and MLS football writer, Karl Matchett, has identified four subjective ways a coach can measure their pressing system:

1. Look at the size and repetition of gap exploited behind the initial press. This can indicate whether one group/area of the team isn't following up the one ahead to keep team compact.

2. A [rough] in-your-head count from the coach of the number of times his team regain possession via the press. Of course, this may not be exact, but it can certainly give a rough estimate over time and could also alert the coach if it's significantly lower in any particular game.

3. Before the game, identify what the press trigger is, and then see whether the players recognize it. Is it moment of transition, is it the opposition crossing a point on pitch (halfway line, center circle, their own 18-yard box…), is it recognizable by the entire team and particularly those who should initiate the press?

4. Maybe most importantly, does the team gain anything tangible by pressing? There is analysis needed in-game or in training sessions to notice if, after pressing and winning the ball, the team is cohesive enough to immediately counter, get a shot/corner/free-kick etc., or whether the press leaves them too tired, too disjointed to really take advantage and begin their own phase of play.

Practice Design

Of course, as coaches we don't need to be convinced about the value of practice and how important it is to players and teams. We learned this optimal strategy at a young age and, because we enjoyed training so much as players, we decided to move onto the coaching side and do it even more. Very few coaches do not have a deep appreciation for work on the training pitch, however, the focus needs to be on how we maximize that time and get our players to learn faster. The more we work at something, the better we should become. Time, focus, type of repetition, and recovery times are all areas that we should be giving serious consideration to during the planning process.

In 'Modern Soccer Coach' I addressed the theory of practice variability on a soccer training model. Nick Winkleman, Head of Athletic Performance and Science with Irish Rugby, developed the concept of 'Perfect Practice Versus Practice Perfectly'. Sometimes as coaches, we fall into a trap of thinking that every exercise must be aesthetically perfect and the session must flow seamlessly together to help the players see the connection between topic and the game. Winkleman, however, challenges us to strengthen the connection between training and the game, and in doing so, stresses the importance of practice variability. Low variability would be doing an exercise in blocks with 30 minutes of 1v1 defending, followed by 30 minutes of 2v2 defending, and then finishing with 30 minutes of 4v4 defending. High variability, on the other hand, would be working on 30 minutes of possession in small areas, followed by 30 minutes of defending in transition, and then finishing with 30 minutes of counter attacking play. By using high variability in your training program, you are changing the theme along with the exercise, and this can be similar to the demands of the game.

The next development is the idea of 'Contextual Interference' which is the application of practice variability. Here, coaches look to take the concept of practice and interfere with it by disrupting accuracy and forcing the player to adapt. In a 1v1 defending exercise where the players are asked to make 50 consecutive defensive actions, the chances are that as time goes on, the players are going to get better at setting their feet and making the challenge because they are experiencing the same scenario over and over again. The same would apply to a passing, shooting or heading exercise. However, what if they had to perform those tasks in a randomized order? As soon as they become comfortable in applying one aspect of technique, the exercise changes and they must adapt quickly. This might well result in a lower level of success in terms of skill execution, but that is not necessarily a bad thing. Over 70% of research looking at a wide range of sports has found a "contextual interference effect", which proves that when you have a higher contextual interference and practice is more random, the transfer and retention of learning those skills is superior.

This theory goes against traditional logic which invariably wants us to reduce mistakes in practice, rather than drill for more. When it comes to coaching pressing, this is an aspect we should seriously consider. In game situations, most pressing mistakes occur in transition when players misread or overlook tactical cues and then take up poor positioning, especially as the game develops. To recreate those situations in training, the exercise must be both multi-functional and/or have a higher level of chaos, where more mistakes will happen but we experience the process and then have the ability to learn from them.

Practice variability also promotes a higher level of adaptability in teams. At the elite level, players will be exposed to playing against different playing systems and different players with non-traditional tendencies. A coaching staff may not have the luxury of preparing their team for these specific challenges so instead must develop players and teams who can adapt and solve problems themselves. A great example of this is Klopp's Liverpool adopting a medium block against Manchester City without instructions from the coach, which we referred to earlier in this book.

At California State University Bakersfield, we use both models. In the pre-season stage, where we want players to gain confidence and an understanding of the specific defensive movements we begin our training model with low levels of variability in sessions. Isolated practices are used to establish the basic fundamentals of our defensive system. With the introduction of new players to the system, we want to give them every chance of being successful. (See following page)

Interactive Session Plan ™

Location: CSUB Women's Soccer   Session date: 8/11/16   Topic: Pressing - Basics in pairs, fours and then positional units

NOTES

4 Groups of Four Players
8 Defending Players in Pairs - Start in middle

Objective: Each pair sprints into box and must win ball in 4v2 situation
After winning ball, must sprint back to square and then to another grid
Each defensive pair must win back 4 balls each
Cannot go to the same grid twice

Basics:
Get there
Apply pressure
Cut off basics
Recover fast

8v4 Keep Ball

4 Defensive players press and four are target players, A-D

White team in possession:
8 passes is one point
8 passes and they can also progress to goal = 2 points

Defensive team must win back 5 balls and get them to the target players A-D
If they miss target players, it doesn't count

Coaching Points:
Work together
Cut off spaces
Find a pass to target in transition

Possession team organized with a GK, Back four, and MF 3

5 White players (Front 3 and 2 MFs) must press continually for 2 mins

If the possession team transfer the ball from one wide area to the other = 1 point

If pressing team win ball and score = 1 point

Coaching Points:
Stopping the switch
Individual roles
Taking advantage of counters

Comments:

Once players are comfortable in roles and responsibilities, we introduce more variability, more mistakes, more learning from mistakes, and better opportunity for learning. With the games now coming thick and fast in our schedule, our goal as a coaching staff is to replicate as many game-like scenarios as we can in our training program.

Interactive Session Plan ™

Location: CSUB Women's Soccer   Session date: 10/4/16   Topic: Play forward in Possession - Press High Without

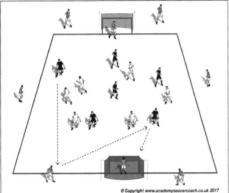

NOTES

3 teams of 6
Must combine with outside players (limited to one touch) to score

Coaching Points:
Defensively - High pressure all over field
Offensively - Get half a yard and try to play forward if possible
Movement of 3rd player to get involved and finish attacks

2 minute games - Winner stays on

Attack v Defense
Front 3 plus 2 supporting mids v Back Four

Back four play long pass into front three of other team in opposite half. Midfielders A and B support to create 5v4

When attack finishes - defensive team must play out under pressure

Coaching Points:
Front three attack, then press the outlet pass - constant work until ball leaves grid
Attacking from central areas - Combinations, 1v1 opportunities, movement off the ball

11v11 Conditioned Game with no restrictions
Scoring System:
Wide Goal - one point (Black Team into A and B, White Team into C and D)
Main Goal - two points

Objective: Apply aggressive pressure in wide areas
Switch point of attack in possession

Coach within the game, no stoppages
Two Sets of 10 minutes

Adding Practice Variability

You can add practice variability to your training program in a couple of different ways. At a younger age, it can be structured in different skill blocks, i.e. dribbling, heading, shooting, etc. When the players have developed and reached the competitive age-group, it becomes a little more complex. Below are three different ways to add this to the program:

Exposure to Game Situations – How does the landscape of the game look and what challenges are your players facing on a consistent basis? For example, the college game is a game of constant transitions, so we look to expose our players to more of those situations than, say for example, patient build-ups or rotation and movement in central midfield.

Sacrifice Perfection – We have addressed this subject of sacrifice on a number of occasions in this book. No matter how you want to defend, you are going to give something up on the other end of the field and potentially leave yourself exposed. The same applies to training if you want to add the concept of variability to your program. Players will be learning in sometimes chaotic situations, and with an increase in tempo and intensity, it could well lead to a drop in technical quality. As a coach, you have to be patient enough to live with the mistakes of the players and then understand that your gains are going to come elsewhere.

Repetition Without Repetition – Repetition is a golden word for a coach, but for today's player it simply means boredom. The challenge for coaches is then to find ways to achieve this repetition, without doing the same thing over and over again. For coaches who are limited with their imagination, I believe this is a lot easier today with more access to online learning and different ideas.

Meeting Physical Demands of the Game

There is no doubt that fatigue is the enemy of consistent pressing, but we have not addressed the specific physical requirements to press effectively in this book for the simple reason that it varies from level to level, and even game to game. It does not take a genius, however, to realize that the fitter your players are, the better chance you will have of implementing any defensive system, particularly a pressing game. We now live in a world where even amateur and youth players have access to excellent facilities and trainers, who can make them fitter and stronger – and coaches should be embracing every resource possible to get additional physical help with their players.

In addition, what coaches should be putting under serious consideration is whether or not our training exercises are challenging players enough on the physical side of the game. Quite simply, are our exercises meeting the demands of the game? Do our players have one action and rest or are they required to perform numerous actions at their maximum? The biggest area of evaluation here is looking at our work to rest ratio. Sometimes an effective pressing exercise can allow players too much time to recover, mentally and physically and consequently fail to challenge them to perform anywhere near their maximum capacity. For example, the following exercise is designed for a central forward pairing (in white) to press against three center backs (in black). Both teams are attempting to score by passing the ball through either of the two goals on the opponent's side of the field. As soon as the ball goes outside the area, a new group of players come on and the current group go back to their starting positions.

It is an exercise where a coach can teach a range of themes including initial pressure, positioning, working together, and transitional defending. One aspect that makes the connection to a game weak is the recovery. Each line contains four players and players are working for a period of 15-20 seconds and then standing still for up to 2 minutes.

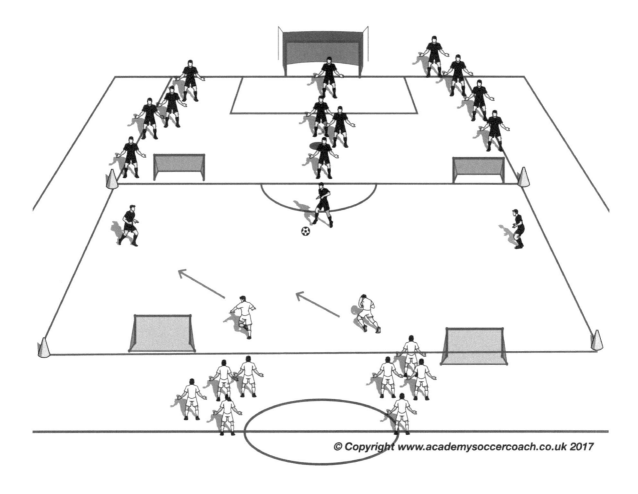

Instead, coaches must challenge their players to extend their periods of extensive work and then learn to perform when they are recovering. The exercise below is an example of the changes you could make to assist with both. The 3v2 exercise that we started with still takes place, however, the coach will now trigger 3 consecutive balls in to increase the volume of work of initial group. After the 3 balls, the next group goes in and the first group recovers. Instead of having five players at each station, another 3v3 game is set up on the opposite side that runs continuously. After 3 minutes, the groups change places and the games continue. The coaches can constantly manipulate the numbers of the game to increase or decrease the physical challenges.

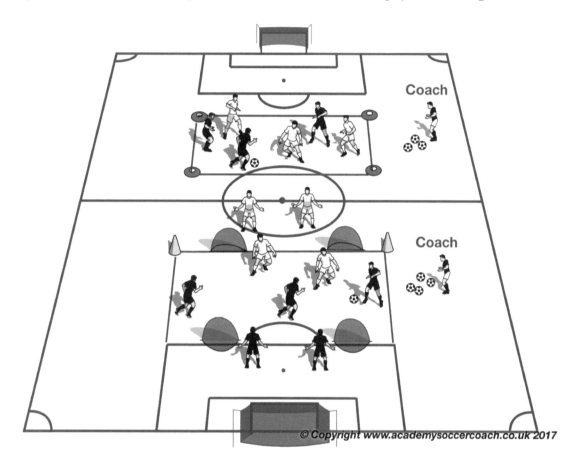

Feedback

Young people today learn best from thinking, not doing. Traditional coaching sessions that simply provide information or in-game coaching that corrects mistakes should now be re-evaluated. Instead we must look for new ways to get players engaged in the defensive side of the game, and our best chance is through video analysis. YouTube has changed the way of learning where now the key to learning is to engage young people's mind. Our goal is then to create an environment where players think, and then develop the ability to manage or predict these situations in a game. More teams today have access to technology and video analysis systems. There is no excuse today for a coach who does not provide constant feedback to their team or players.

Individual Video Analysis

"The more you can involve your players and the more you can get them to tell you what they are doing, the better. Don't fall into the trap of thinking that you're doing good work and they are nodding their heads. Don't believe them. Only believe them when they tell you." – Roy Hodgson

When a pressing system fails, it is normally down to one mistake. Very rarely will 3 or more players be out of position and then the defensive structure of the team crumbles. At the highest levels, individual defensive mistakes make the difference. Therefore, when it comes to developing better defensive teams, we must start by creating better defensive players alongside better units and teams. Why should we replicate traditional ways of delivering feedback, simply because it's time efficient and includes everyone? When comparing a coach-driven model against one built around co-ownership, former Tottenham Hotspur and Leicester City Head of Technical Scouting, Rob McKenzie, believes that because players are constantly told what to do, they are not equipped to solve problems or deal with anything other than the proposed scenario and solution. To highlight this problem, he used the example of a GPS system in a car. When players are receiving instructions every day from the coach they become reliant on it and have no ownership. Then if an 'accident' or 'diversion' occurs during the game, the players invariably get lost.

Learning for players is very much experience based and Mackenzie identified four principles that must be present for this learning to occur:

1. It has to mean something to the individual.
2. Individual must have perceived ownership.
3. It must be planned with structured actions and thoughts.
4. The player must have the capacity and willingness to learn.

In addition, individual video analysis provides the following benefits to players and coaches:

Saves Time – If there is a mistake in training, the session does not have to stop for the coach to address it with a certain player. It can be reviewed later in a less pressurized environment where the player can also give his/her input.

Dialogue Over Monologue – Addressing an individual defensive mistake in front of the team in a locker room, meeting room, or on a training pitch will typically lead to the same reaction from the player in question. They will agree with the coach and hope that the spotlight moves on to someone else quickly. Coaches today must remove social consequences attached to feedback and learn to deliver it in a more effective way.

Builds Trust – Eddie Howe feels that individual sessions enable the coach to strengthen the relationship with the players. "I'll always do the feedback on an individual basis. I don't believe in doing it together because I think you can't then be really truthful and honest. Not that it's negative. I'm trying to make it educational. It's basically saying: 'I really liked this, I didn't quite like this.' It's probably my biggest drain in terms of time, but I think it's one of the most important aspects that I do."

Enhances Quality of Information – Many times as coaches we dump large amounts of information on a player during a session without ever checking to see how it is received. We must remove the assumption that players understand and retain everything we say and instead involve them further in the communication process so that we can gauge what they learn and what they need.

Drives Accountability – One area where the game has not changed is every player wanting to be on that pitch during the game. With squad sizes increasing, this can be a challenging time for a coach. Middlesbrough boss, Aitor Karanka, believes that video is one of the best ways to explain a coaching decision or playing time to a player. "If a player knocks on my door, and it's always open, and asks why he is not starting, I have a thousand videos to show why. It shocks the players. They never imagine that you have so much information."

Summary

- ✓ Coaching is no longer instructing players to carry out instructions. How we communicate is now more important than what we communicate.

- ✓ Pressing is more than hard work and commitment. In many cases, it's problem solving and finding solutions during games, both individually and collectively. Therefore, we must look into how we can impact these areas with our coaching.

- ✓ Character cannot be compromised and must be evaluated as part of the recruiting process. It is a crucial piece in building the right culture. A difficult opponent beats you every once in a while, but a difficult teammate beats you every day.

- ✓ How players conduct themselves off the field is typically how they conduct themselves on it.

- ✓ When working with millennials, part of the adaptive process for coaches is getting outside of the orbit of your own experience and entering the world in which they live. It is our responsibility to reach out, connect, and attempt to make a difference.

- ✓ A coach's body language speaks louder than their words. Find a balance on the touchline between driving energy that your players will require to sustain repeated high levels of intensity, and giving them space to solve problems and express themselves. This should be a work-in-progress at all times.

- ✓ Find a way to evaluate your press that goes beyond results, distances, or comparing it to spaces conceded in other teams. Make it specific to your team and allow it to give your players constant feedback on their development.

- ✓ Once players have a base level of understanding, practice variability can help players meet the demands of the game quicker, strengthen their learning, and promote higher levels of adaptability in teams.

✓ Practice organization is critical in establishing pressing exercises that challenge players to mentally and physically recover as quickly as they will be required to in games.

✓ Individual video analysis increases the possibility of creating a co-ownership model with players that will build trust, drive accountability, enhance the quality of information given, and increase their emotional buy-in to the team.

Final Thoughts

At the time I began writing this book two years ago, I decided to implement the same model and philosophies with my college team, California State University, Bakersfield. We initially wanted to design a system of play that would match the youthful exuberance of our team. What would get our players excited about fighting for the jersey and competing every weekend? Pressing seemed to suit our desired self-image and therefore became a focal point in our play model. Alongside it our staff used, and are still using, the player profiles that we created in every position to drive our recruitment. In addition, the work on culture and creating an environment where players are willing to go above and beyond for each other is still very much a work in progress, but has been an area of great improvement. In summary, I think that success in pressing revolves around the 3 T's.

Traditional

When we began implementing a pressing system, we found that the best way to do this was to identify easy triggers which could allow us to press aggressively as a team. The traditional pressing markers are not very complex and occur when our opponents are starting their build-up in possession. For example, we expect our team to be well organized during opposing goal kicks, throw-ins deep in the opponent's half, and when any of their back four are in possession of the ball. When these situations occur, we are conditioned mentally and physically to understand roles and responsibilities, and implement them at speed.

Transitional

The college game is all about transitions. It can be played at a hectic pace and, with the emotional card of a three-month season creating a 'Cup Final' atmosphere every Friday night, even the best teams will make a number of mistakes in possession. We want our players to focus on the reaction rather than the mistake and look to capitalize on opponents who have not yet regained control of the ball. Working hard on this side of the game has allowed us to take more risks in possession and conceding less goals as a result of counter attacks.

Transformational

Without doubt, this is the hardest aspect to coach and implement with our team and is still very much in the growth stage. When the conditions of the game change, e.g. score, fatigue, time, etc., we want to be able to adapt our pressing system and change effectively. Our goal would be to change the defensive system without a half-time break or a series of substitutions and believe that if we could do that, we could regain control of the game a lot quicker if it starts to slip. We want our players to be decision makers in this process and learn to read the flow of the game. Our main areas of work here have been through video feedback and developing leaders who can communicate effectively in the heat of a game.

As our team continues to grow and develop, we are doing the same with the coaching staff. We are constantly looking for ways to improve and challenge our players, knowing that we are limited only by our desire to learn more. I urge every coach to do the same and share the experience with the coaching community. Like everything in the game, we don't learn from taking a specific model and implementing it with our team, but instead by tailoring it to suit the needs of our players and the environment we want to create. I wish every coach the best of luck in this special process!

Recommended Reading

'What Is Tactical Periodization' by Xavier Tamarit

'Tactical Periodisation' by Pedro Mendonca

'Pep Confidential' by Marti Perarnau

About the Author

Gary Curneen is the Head Women's Soccer Coach at California State University Bakersfield. Gary holds a UEFA 'A' License from the Irish FA and a "Premier Diploma" from the NSCAA. Gary also gained a Master's in Business Administration from Wingate University, where he was the Head Women's Soccer Coach from 2005-2013, taking them to the NCAA Tournament for the first time in the program's history.

Gary has played and coached at the collegiate level in the United States for more than ten years. His coaching education has seen him travel to study the best teams in the world and how they work first hand. A lifelong learner, Gary is a player- centered coach who focuses on professionalism, responsibility, and accountability within the framework of each team he works with. He believes that creating a culture of excellence is paramount to success and that each training session should include physical, tactical, technical, and mental components that challenge the players to perform at a high level.